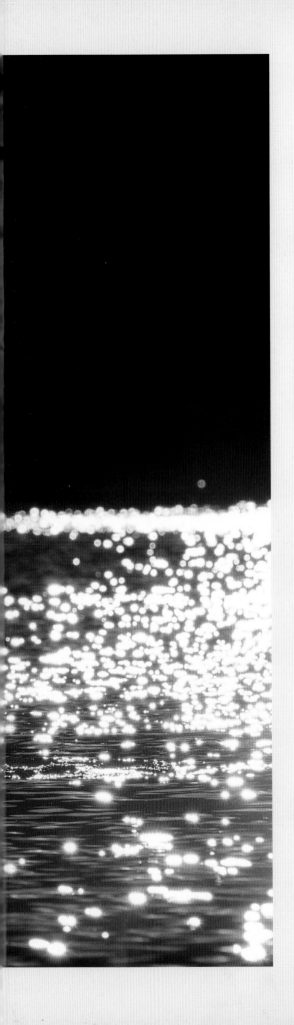

Moose

◆ Behavior ◆ Ecology
◆ Conservation

By Valerius Geist
Photography by Michael H. Francis
Foreword by Dr. Robert Wegner

Voyageur Press

Dedication

To Alain Deschamps

Acknowledgements

I am grateful to Jim Peek of the University of Idaho for reading and commenting on this manuscript; to Reinhold Eben-Ebenau of Lesser Slave Lake, Alberta, for his generous help with literature and the discussions we had; to Ralph Ritzey and York Edwards who started it all in 1959; and to my infinitely patient and ever constructive Renate.

Text copyright © 1999 by Valerius Geist
Photographs copyright © 1999 by Michael H. Francis

Edited by Jane Billinghurst
Designed by Andrea Rud
Printed in Hong Kong

99 00 01 02 03 5 4 3 2 1

Library of Congress Cataloging-in-Publication Data
  Geist, Valerius.
    Moose : behavior, ecology, conservation / text by Valerius Geist ; photography by Michael H. Francis.
        p.   cm.
    Includes bibliographical references.
    ISBN 0-89658-422-4
    1. Moose. I. Francis, Michael H. (Michael Harlowe), 1953-   .
  II. Title.
  QL737.U55G426   1999
  599.65'7—dc21   99-24769
                              CIP

Distributed in Canada by Raincoast Books, 8680 Cambie Street, Vancouver, B.C. V6P 6M9

Published by Voyageur Press, Inc.
123 North Second Street, P.O. Box 338, Stillwater, MN 55082 U.S.A.
651-430-2210, fax 651-430-2211

Educators, fundraisers, premium and gift buyers, publicists, and marketing managers: Looking for creative products and new sales ideas? Voyageur Press books are available at special discounts when purchased in quantities, and special editions can be created to your specifications. For details contact the marketing department at 800-888-9653.

PAGE 1: The Grand Tetons in Wyoming make a fine backdrop to an exceptional sagebrush bull of the Shirasi ecotype.
PAGES 2–3: A bull in velvet feeds from a pond.
FACING PAGE: A cow comes to a Maine lake for water.
PAGE 6–7: A bull moves through a morning blanket of fog in Yellowstone National Park in Wyoming.

Contents

Foreword

By Dr. Robert Wegner

Valerius Geist is not only one of the finest popularizers of science, but he is the most enthusiastic deer researcher to emerge in the last century. His enthusiasm for deer behavior is infectious. In his lectures and published works, Professor Geist shares a tremendous wealth of information about all members of the deer family. This great "deer man," this joyous original thinker, studies and reports on deer behavior in several languages.

Born in Nikoljew, USSR, in 1938, Valerius Geist studies animal behavior with a cross-cultural perspective, tracing the relationship the animal maintains with people from the perspective of world history. He received his Ph.D. in zoology in 1966 from the University of British Columbia, where he studied under Dr. Ian McTaggert-Cowan.

After spending a year of postdoctoral study with Konrad Lorenz in Germany, Professor Geist joined the University of Calgary, where he cofounded the faculty of Environmental Design. There he served as the first program director for Environmental Sciences. His scientific work on the biology and evolution of large Ice Age mammals has been honored by the Wildlife Society, the Foundation for North American Wild Sheep, and the American Association for the Advancement of Science.

Whether working as a film consultant, serving as an expert witness in investigations dealing with illegal conservation practices, or debating with deer biologists over the controversies involved with game ranching, Geist is a true friend of the deer family. Indeed, he is a master at writing blue-chip deer books for the popular domain.

A bull performing a lip-curl. Lip-curling is performed by bulls on female urine during the mating season to see if the cows are approaching ovulation.

I do not know of a better teacher and author on the subject matter of deer behavior, ecology, evolution, management, and public policy than this renowned scientist, keen observer, and natural storyteller. He speaks and writes with profound conviction and unmistakable passion based on in-depth scientific study and historical analysis.

Geist's style has been characterized by editor Dick McCabe of the Wildlife Management Institute as a blend of "hard European science and New World popular prose." When he speaks and writes about the mysteries of deer behavior, I listen and read with great interest. His deep-digging research challenges the student of deer behavior to the ultimate limits.

Geist stands in the company of the great deer men of all time, men who made significant contributions towards understanding these animals: Ernest Thompson Seton, Judge Caton, F. Fraser Darling, and Aldo Leopold. Like Aldo Leopold, Geist popularizes his own scientific studies and serves as his own best critic. In the preface to the classic book *Mountain Sheep: A Study in Behavior and Evolution*, published in 1971, he writes: "At present my graduate students and I are working hard to make this book obsolete." Like Aldo Leopold, Geist combines the excitement of field research and intellectual discovery with basic scientific principles.

This beautiful book filled with spectacular color photographs splendidly captures the world and soul of the moose, that magnificent animal that scientist Tony Bubenik calls "the mighty monarch of the taiga."

Dr. Robert Wegner
Author of *Deer and Deer Hunting*, volumes 1–3

This bull of the eastern form of moose sports the typical bull bell, which consists of a broad fold of skin that reaches from the level of the corner of the mouth to the angle of the lower jaw. Cows normally lack this bag.

Prologue

The Super Cub banked around the snowy mountainside. I was packed in grizzly bear fur, huddled behind the pilot of the tiny aircraft. Even the heavy fur gave scant comfort in the icy air of this brilliant December day in Canada's southern Yukon. Stone's sheep and mountain goats had left tracks and feeding craters in the snow below. Disturbed by the sound of the plane's engines, a flock of white ptarmigan burst from hiding and curved into the dark shadows of a canyon. As we skimmed over a lake's forested edge, a group of mountain caribou ran out onto the ice; six wolves in a clearing scattered and dove for cover under the surrounding pines. We turned and climbed over a long mountain ridge above the timberline. Minutes later, we spied a group of seven majestic bull moose, each carrying a set of huge, widely spreading antlers. They glanced up from feeding in the dense willows as we floated by. We slid towards the broad valley of the Wolf River and we spied more moose: cows isolated with their calves, a huge bull or two, lone moose in willow creeks or on the sites of old forest fires. Low on the slopes of the mountain range, a bundle of specks gradually transformed into a gathering of nineteen young bull moose. Two pairs of these juveniles were engaged in friendly sparring matches. I recorded their presence and moved on, satisfied with what I had seen.

A mature young bull feeds in a Maine pond in early July. Aquatic feeding is common for moose in eastern and northern North America, yet uncommon in western moose. One prevailing hypothesis is that aquatic vegetation is rich in sodium salts, and so compensates for a lack of mineral licks.

How the Moose Got Its Big Nose

The moose is the largest living member of the deer family. Moose are found in northern North America and throughout northern Eurasia from Scandinavia to eastern Siberia. As the result of policies and laws that have protected moose and recognized them as a valuable natural resource, moose have expanded their geographic range greatly in the past century. Great explorers and colonizers when left to their own devices, moose have also been transplanted by wildlife managers beyond their native range into areas such as Utah and Colorado in the southern Rocky Mountain states, or into Newfoundland in eastern Canada. In regions of Europe and Siberia moose numbers have also increased.

A Maine bull approaches a young bull slowly and deliberately in a dominance display. The antlers of an exceptional bull moose today may exceed seven feet (2.1 m) in spread. However, the antlers of the mid–Ice Age ancestor of moose, *Alces latifrons*, may have doubled in spread and mass even those of the largest Alaskan bulls.

Moose are largest in Alaska and eastern Siberia, where old bulls weigh 1,200 to 1,400 pounds (545–636 kg) and occasionally even more. Across their range, moose decline in size from the 65th parallel southward, to reach a body weight of 550 to 800 pounds (250–363 kg) at the 40th parallel. There are exceptions to the pattern, however: when moose colonize particularly rich feeding areas, southern moose of modest size may grow to rival their Alaskan counterparts. As a rule of thumb, where moose colonize fertile new feeding areas, they are large; where they exploit ecologically mature flora in established populations, they are small. And that is the key to the many subspecies that have been described for moose.

Biologists gave moose in different regions different taxonomic names if they differed in size and proportions. Thus we have in North America, the Shiras moose (*Alces alces shirasi* Nelson, 1914) to the south of moose range, the Alaskan moose (*Alces alces gigas* Miller, 1899) to the north, the Eastern moose in the east (*Alces alces americanus* Clinton, 1822), and the North-Western moose (*Alces alces andersoni* Peterson, 1950) in between the three others. These names look impressive; however, they do not reflect knowledge about moose, but ignorance. This naming goes back to an era when biologists paid little attention to how mammals change in size and proportions under environmental influences, even though animal scientists working in the applied discipline of agriculture were aware of these changes. Body size and proportions change together, and both are sensitive to the nutritional regimes of the individual. Whatever an animal's genetic potential, its body size is much influenced by its environment.

The giant moose of the Alaska Peninsula is large because the region experiences a long period of intense plant production from spring to fall, fueled by the long hours of summer sunshine at that latitude. Long hours of sunshine, followed by brief, cool nights, greatly enhance photosynthesis and the retention of carbohydrates and protein in plants, while slowing fiber deposition. This makes plants highly digestible and nutritious. Moreover, moose colonized Alaska relatively recently, and so the vegetation is not conditioned to moose browsing and the plants have not developed defenses against being eaten. The more large herbivores crop plants, the more they stimulate plant defenses. Plants usually defend themselves by depositing increased levels of toxins in their leaves and bark. Plants that are not browsed and therefore do not need to defend themselves shift their energy from defense to reproduction and thus are more digestible.

On average, the largest moose around the world reside between the 60th and 65th parallels. Above and below these latitudes, body size declines. Above the 65th parallel summers are short, and there are too few days of abundant food supply to allow herbivores to grow large. Below the 65th parallel, warm temperatures and increasingly fewer hours of sunshine per day insure rapid maturation of plants. At these latitudes herbs and woody plants do not remain young and digestible for long. They quickly grow toxic and fibrous, which makes them more difficult to eat.

Recent studies indicate little genetic variation in moose in different regions. The Shiras moose and the giant moose of Alaska are good examples of ecotypes—that is to say, variations generated by different environments—but they are not separate subspecies. Despite the many different names given to moose by biologists, there are only two good subspecies in the world today: the European/West Siberian moose (*Alces alces alces* Linnaeus, 1758) and the East Siberian/North American moose (*Alces alces americanus* Clinton, 1822).

Moose not only vary in size regionally; they also vary in color. Moose that live in the deep forests of eastern North America tend to be dark; those that live in the more exposed regions of the West and North are lighter and more colorful. The more a moose is exposed to direct sunlight, the more likely it is to have a light saddle marking on its back. This saddle also occurs on other large mammals, such as grizzly bears, elk, bison, and musk oxen. The best

A Maine bull with a typical bull bell, which has been trimmed in length by freezing in severe winter cold spells. In North America, the sex of a moose can be determined by the color of its nose. Cow moose have reddish brown noses, whereas bulls have black ones.

current explanation is that wherever large mammals have to exert themselves in the open in intense sunlight in summer or early fall, it pays to have a reflective shield on the back so as to absorb as little solar heat as possible during vigorous activities. For most ungulates that means the elevated activity, particularly in males, at mating time. Ungulates that mate in cool or cold fall and winter weather—such as caribou, mountain sheep, and deer—do not have these light saddles. Large mammals that can take advantage of the shadow of trees in summer are also less in need of a body color that reflects heat, which is why moose that favor deep forest habitat are darker than moose that live in more exposed conditions. Having said that, there is so much individual variation in coat color among moose that one cannot tell from the color of its coat where an individual moose comes from—other than to identify it as either a European or a North American moose. Unlike elk or deer, which have a separate red summer and distinct nuptial or winter coat, moose replace their long winter coat with another winter coat. That is, they do not grow a separate, distinct summer coat.

The Evolution of Moose

The most distinguishing feature of the moose is, of course, its nose. We make fun of it and cartoonists lampoon it mercilessly. It is unconventional in shape and distressingly complex in anatomy. Dissect this big nose and one bogs down in a multitude of crisscrossing muscles and nerve fibers. This suggests that the muzzle is very mobile, and one does not need anatomical evidence to come to that conclusion. A few minutes of watching a feeding moose feed will do. A moose uses its nose to test the pliability of twigs on trees and bushes. Nutritious young twigs are pliable; less nutritious older twigs are not. The complexity of the moose nose also suggests that it can gather a great deal of information about the moose's surroundings. Moose have a keen sense of smell and the nostrils are spaced so far apart that some three-dimensional "smell imagery" may well be possible. The complex inner channeling of the muzzle may also have something to do with feeding on aquatic plants underwater. All deer can pluck aquatic vegetation from water, but to swallow they must raise

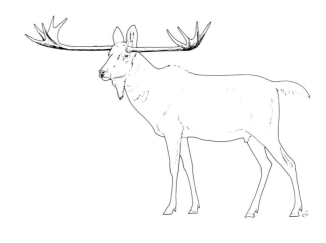

The earliest moose (*Libralces gallicus*) might have looked like this. It had the face of a deer and the body of a plains runner. It was about the size of a small bull elk and its antlers were decidedly odd. It lived 2.6 million years ago, probably in the open savannas of Europe.

The extinct American moose *Cervalces scotti* being chased by a giant short-faced bear (*Arctodus simus*). This moose was as large as the largest Alaskan moose today and had much larger and more complex antlers. Its body identifies it as a long-legged trotter with large, widely splaying hooves designed for life in the shallows of the immense pro-glacial lakes that marked the interior of Pleistocene North America. Both animals died out at the end of the last Ice Age, about ten to twelve thousand years ago.

FACING PAGE: A bull performing a lip-curl.

A bull in early September in Yellowstone National Park. The moose of eastern North America are, in general, smaller and darker than Alaskan moose, but larger in body and antler size than moose from Wyoming and Montana. Genetically the moose of North America differ from Eastern Siberian moose so little as to be the same subspecies. Regional differences are ecotypic, that is, due to different food and climatic conditions for growth and development. Modern moose entered North America from eastern Siberia barely ten thousand years ago.

their heads out of the water. A moose can feed efficiently underwater because it does not need to raise its head with every bite. Just how this complex natural machinery actually works, however, is a puzzle.

The muzzle of a moose is wonderfully soft and sensitive, a prime organ for exploration, and so different from the noses of other deer. Yet, long ago, the moose did have a nose just like other deer. The most ancient moose on record, *Libralces gallicus*, had a head and snout much like a conventional deer. It lived in Europe about 2.6 million years ago. It was about the size of a small bulk elk today. It had smaller teeth than today's moose, and its body was built for fast running on reasonably long legs. It also had distinctive, wide-spreading antlers. *Libralces* probably lived in an open savanna and bush steppe in a temperate climate, feeding on young grasses, herbaceous plants or forbs, some foliage, and browse. There is not a shred of evidence for a "moose nose" for the next two million years.

In the early to mid-Pleistocene epoch, about 700,000 to 900,000 years ago, moose reappeared on the paleontological scene, this time as giants. These giant moose were one of a number of species of Asiatic fauna that appeared in Europe in the warm periods between successive ice ages. These huge moose—known as broad-fronted moose because of their sturdy, broad skulls—had long legs and stood as tall at the shoulders as any large Alaskan moose today. Their teeth were like those of today's moose, only much larger. The broad-fronted moose was clearly a browser, a shredder of woody twigs. Its nose was still elegantly deerlike, but more innervated and a little enlarged. That is not surprising, as enlarged lips and mobile noses are common in specialized foliage feeders and browsers. It suggests only that after millions of years with the face of a conventional deer and probably a highly successful mixed feeding strategy moose were beginning to specialize in their feeding habits.

The changes in the body size and skull structure of the broad-fronted moose were accompanied by a change in antlers. In speedy runners on open plains that are much tested by fast predators, newborns need to be large and advanced in development at birth to keep up with their mothers in flight. There-

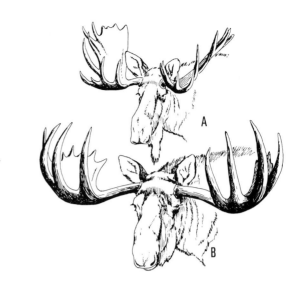

A modern Alaskan moose (A) and its Eurasian mid-Pleistocene predecessor, the broad-fronted moose (B), which may have had twice the body mass of the largest modern moose.

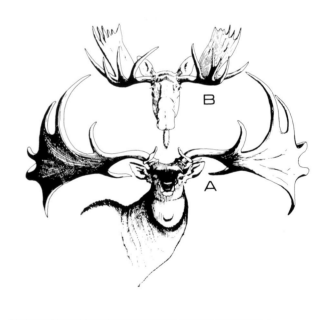

The giant Irish elk, *Megaloceros* (A), had about the same body mass as a large modern moose (B), but it had twice the antler mass.

22

fore these females shift a large portion of their energy resources into reproduction. Not only must the babies be quick and large, but they must also grow rapidly after birth so as to match adults in running speed and endurance. Consequently, the females must produce much rich milk. Which fathers should such females choose so that their daughters can produce a maximum quantity of rich milk, as well as bear big, advanced babies? The answer is the males with the largest "luxury organs." Male deer deposit excess nutrients into their antlers. An impressive display of antlers attests to their superior ability to find food. In species where males sport big antlers or horns, the females produce big babies and rich milk—and the males show off their luxury organs to the females during courtship. This indicates that the females in fleet-footed, large-antlered forms of deer choose the males they accept as the fathers of their children. Since the long, thin-beamed antlers of *Libralces* were more for show than for fighting, this suggests that these small moose were adapted to open landscapes where females could select for males of their choice based on antler size.

In small-antlered, forest-dwelling species of deer, females have little choice in who their mates are and males gain access to females by violence. The broad-fronted moose had antlers with smaller beams but larger palms and longer tines than those of its predecessor. The large absolute size but relatively small mass of the antlers of broad-fronted moose suggests that these moose were increasingly relying on cover. Moose were heading away from open terrain, towards more broken ground, with an emphasis on foliage feeding and browsing over feeding on meadow forbs and grasses. At the same time, they were evolving a new security strategy, one of trotting with little body lift over low obstacles, which forced pursuing wolves or bears to either run around or jump over these obstacles. Either method of pursuit would tire the predators out or slow them down.

Virtually all species of herbi-

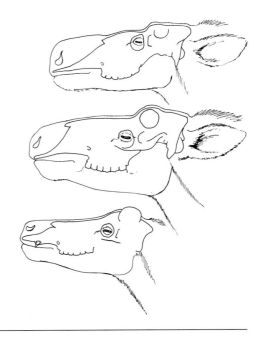

ABOVE: The evolution of the moose nose. Bottom: *Libralces gallicus* (2.6 million years old). Middle: *Cervalces scotti* (the extinct American moose; 0.5 million years old). Top: modern moose. Only the modern moose shows the distinctive moose nose; earlier moose were not so specialized.

BELOW: The differences between European moose (A) and North American moose (B) are shown in these illustrations. American moose have a distinctive light saddle marking over their backs, and darker leg and facial markings. The two moose also differ in the size of their antlers. European bull moose carry half the antler mass of North American bulls, and their antlers have three prongs rather than four.

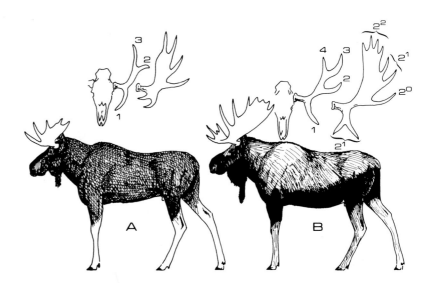

23

ABOVE: A well-grown calf moose moves through Jasper National Park in Alberta, Canada, in the autumn. It has assumed the adult, dark-hair coat.

RIGHT: A bull moose shrouded by the morning mist.

Moose feed in a regular daily rhythm. When food is abundant, the feeding periods are short and the moose feeds often during the day. When food is scarce and hard to digest, the feeding and resting periods are extended. Moose are not always early risers, but they do have a rather high activity peak at dusk. Otherwise, there are normally several feeding peaks during the day, four in late spring—but only one in January. In summer, moose visit favored feeding sites any time of the day. Only where severely disturbed are moose secretive and nocturnal.

vores and carnivores that appeared in Eurasia in the early to mid-Pleistocene along with the broad-fronted moose were exceptionally large in body size—then all species began to shrink. This reduction in body size suggests that there was a reproductive reward for living and successfully reproducing on less food. With many large animals around, high-quality food would be in short supply. If food was in short supply, another sign to look for besides dwarfing is the specialization of feeding organs. Indeed, the wooly mammoth, while shrinking in size, evolved progressively more complex teeth to shred vegetation more efficiently. It was the same with horses and, to a certain extent, with giant deer; however, the same trend is not evident in broad-fronted moose. Their teeth did not enlarge or become more complex as their

body size decreased. In fact, tooth size shrinks from ancient to modern moose. Was the moose an exception to the general trend?

Contrasting the fates of moose that stayed in Eurasia with early moose that traveled to North America across the Bering land bridge about 300,000 years ago provides a hint at what was going on. The moose that crossed to North America became known as the American stag moose or *Cervalces scotti*. It became smaller but not nearly as small as the broad-fronted moose in Eurasia. Its legs grew longer. Its antlers increased in mass and complexity, but the bone structure to support their use shrank in size. Whereas the body and antlers of this American moose changed dramatically, its skull did not. Something similar happened to other herbivores that en-

A wet cow in late June in the midst of shedding her winter hair coat and growing a new one. Note that she has no bell, except for some long hair on the nape.

tered North America during the Pleistocene. The species ballooned in size and their teeth remained surprisingly primitive, while those of their ever-smaller brethren in Europe become increasingly complex.

Collectively the changes undergone by herbivores in North America indicate that they landed in a hellhole of predation. The predators were large bodied, highly specialized in limbs and dentition, and chronically short of food. To survive these ever-hungry predators, *Cervalces* perfected speedy running over low obstacles and good footing on swampy terrain. It was almost certainly under pressure to bear larger calves at birth and to produce richer milk so that the calves might rapidly grow to survivable size. It would, consequently, have been under severe sexual selection for larger antlers. Consequently, *Cervalces* bulls probably relied less on violence than on a show

of antlers to succeed in mating, and so there was little need for massive neck bones. Where there are many fierce and resourceful predators, the density of prey is likely to be low. Where there is a low population density, those who escape from predators can enjoy an abundance of nutritious forage that is relatively easy to digest. The survivors do not need highly specialized teeth or specialized feeding organs or better methods of finding food. Thus the large body and antler size and relatively unspecialized feeding organs of *Cervalces* were the product of the predator-limited fauna of Pleistocene North America.

In Pleistocene Eurasia, however, predators were less successful, and the number and density of herbivores was relatively high. Chronic food shortages led to improvements in teeth and other feeding organs, and to selection for smaller body sizes that could survive on less or on poorer food. In the resource-limited fauna of Eurasia, herbivores ate more second- and third-rate food, which made greater demands on their teeth. An alternative to competing with other herbivores for low-quality forage was to seek out foods previously underused because they were difficult to eat. Rather than becoming better at grinding coarse-fibered browse, as many of the Pleistocene herbivores in Eurasia choose to do, the broad-fronted moose added aquatic plants to its diet. This required a special feeding organ and that is the origin of the "moose nose" and one reason moose teeth did not evolve in the same way as the teeth of the wooly mammoth, the horse, and some other species of deer.

Cervalces with the small, primitive nose disappeared from North America about 10,500 years ago, to be replaced by the Eurasian moose with the big specialized nose, which traveled across the Bering land bridge to Alaska about 10,000 years ago. The two subspecies of advanced moose we know today are thus closely related and their habits and lifestyles are similar in both North America and Eurasia.

There are two subfamilies of deer in the world today: New World deer and Old World deer. The two subfamilies differ in foot structure in that the last remnants of the second and fifth metapodial leg bones are retained as splinters in the lower part of the foot in New World deer and in the upper part of the foot in Old World deer. The Old World deer trace back in the fossil record to the Old World tropics, where we find today the most primitive of their kind. The origins of New World deer are less clear. The circumstantial evidence suggests that they arose about four to six million years ago in both far northern North America and Siberia. New World deer, the white-tailed deer among them, appeared abruptly in

A big bull calling. This rutting male has a drawn-in belly, a sign that he has restricted feeding in favor of roaming, courting, and challenging rivals. Bulls call primarily when courting females, and the cows may reply with similar sounds. Bulls also call—in a similar voice—when approaching rivals, but they space the calls farther apart, emphasizing exhaling. They may, for instance, call as each left front hoof strikes the ground. Because the approach in dominance display is slow and deliberate, the calls are well spaced.

Cow and calf of the light-colored
Alaska moose in early fall.

lower North America as the late Tertiary climate cooled with the approach of the ice ages. Then, as South America touched North America, they quickly moved south and diversified. Simultaneously the moose appeared in the colder latitudes of Europe, followed by the reindeer and the roe deer. The elk is a classic Old World deer, and the only one of its kind to cross into North America. Other Old World deer include the red and fallow deer, the tropical rusas, sambar, hog, and axis deer, as well as the diminutive, ancient muntjac deer. The extinct American and today's modern moose are both New World deer, as are all other deer found in North America.

ABOVE: A big rutting bull surveys his domain for rivals and mates. This is a huge, prime Alaskan bull, the largest current specimen of the entire deer family. Even the giant Irish elk matched, but did not surpass, large Alaskan moose in size. Only the mid-Pleistocene ancestors of current moose were bigger. Reconstructions suggest they were twice the mass of Alaskan bulls, and 1.25 times longer in linear dimensions.

FACING PAGE: Moose depend on snow for survival. Loose snow insulates against the cold, and moose love to slump into deep loose snow—like the cow in the foreground. The long hair of moose insulates well. Note the unmelted snow on the back of the calf. In deep cold, rather thick willow stems lose their elasticity, which allows moose to break them with little effort and to feed on the numerous terminal twigs.

The bell of the bull differs from that of the cow. Bulls have a bag with a rope dangling from its rear margins; cows have a rope only, and occasionally no bell at all. The bell is a skin fold covered by long hair. It is covered by the moose with urine-soaked mud during the rut and serves as a scent dispenser, much as the long neck hair of bull elk does. Note the light hair on the neck, withers, and rump of this bull. This is typical of American, but not European, moose.

ABOVE: Black flies swarm around moose. These blood-sucking, tissue-ripping insects in the north also have a short season in which to reproduce. Little wonder that they avail themselves of opportunities to feed, as the window of opportunity is woefully narrow. Moose attract horse flies, deer flies, stable flies, mosquitoes, black flies, biting midges, nose bot warbles—in addition to other parasites. Clouds of biting insects not only hover above a feeding moose, but even over the spot where a moose dives for food in a pond, waiting for the animal to surface.

RIGHT: A friendly sparring match between greatly unequal bulls. In these sporting engagements hard rules prevail, so that the smaller animal does not suffer. Sparring is common; fighting is rare—and engaged in only by bulls of equal size.

Antler Development

After shedding antlers between mid-December and January, bull moose put antler growth on hold until mid- to late April.

Antler buds begin to grow again from the healed antler pedicles. To grow large antlers, bulls must be in good body condition at the time of antler growth. They are able to raid their bones and body stores for nutrients and energy to accelerate antler growth.

Once started, antlers grow rapidly. By late May, old bulls already have velvet-covered palms.

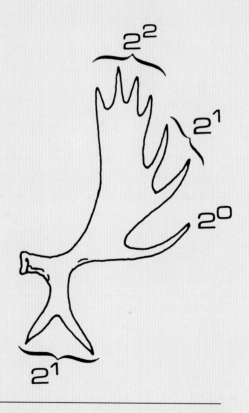

Moose antlers tend to branch in a mathematical fashion. The first tine branches once (2^1), the second stays undivided (2^0), the third tine branches once (2^1), and the fourth tine branches twice (2^2).

Antler growth is completed by the end of August, about 150 days after it began. Then the velvet dies, apparently causing some irritation to the bulls, which busily begin to horn shrubs and small trees to rid the new antlers of velvet. This takes only a few days before the new antlers take on their mature appearance.

The velvet is sensitive. It is well innervated and supplied with a dense network of blood vessels. The growth of large palms may be followed virtually day by day.

The Great Shuttle Between Habitats

Late spring, after the snow has melted and just before the trees leaf out, is a good time to get to know moose. True, they do not look their best at this time of the year. Antlers in early growth stick out like dark stumps from the heads of the bulls. All are gaunt, having lost much weight during winter, and their coats are badly worn, giving them a moth-eaten appearance; however, in terms of behavior there is much to see. In spring and early summer the bulls congregate, and the cows search out places to calve and to rid themselves of last year's yearlings. The days are long, the sun shines, and one can see well through the bare branches of the shrubs and trees.

At high elevations, plants are exceptionally nutritious. Moose feeding on sprouting leaves and flowers select food of the highest quality—essential for the growth of antlers, but also for the hair coat and the restoration of the body after a winter's harshness.

The gray dawn of a late spring day may find moose snoozing in sedge meadows. They are usually alone, but occasionally mature bulls whose antlers have just started to grow form small groups. As the daylight advances, the moose stir in anticipation of rising. They are in no hurry to terminate their snooze. Eventually, after getting up, moose stretch—in slow motion—and then, after a restful pause, scratch themselves. Bulls rub the buds of their antlers against their raised hind legs—apparently the growing points on the antlers itch a little. In the pause between resting and feeding, the moose scratch, urinate, and defecate. Having completed their morning toilet, they proceed to fill up with food. The majority are feeding by about 6:00 a.m. Feeding lasts about an hour, then most moose are down again, taking another snooze. After all, the point so early in spring is to add mass to the depleted muscle, to resolidify porous bone, to deposit layers of fat, to grow sturdy antlers or embryos, and to shed the old, badly worn coat and replace it with a shiny, new one. All that is exhausting enough in itself. It is also terribly important to ensure the moose are fit for breeding later in fall. Consequently, the output of energy is minimized so as to increase body growth.

Large amounts of energy and diverse nutrients are required to restore the body after the hardships of winter, and moose are in constant search of superior food. They can be found browsing adjacent to the timberline in the Arctic and traveling along the shores of the Arctic Ocean in the Yukon. They live along the fertile floodplains of rivers, and in deltas where rivers and creeks enter lakes. They thrive on old burns left by fires in the boreal forest or taiga and on clearcuts. They are at home in the mountains of western North America and northern Eurasia, wandering from subalpine meadows to the valley floors. Some North American moose winter in the sagebrush flats of the western United States, and some European moose find the commercial pine forests of Scandinavia to their liking.

The Importance of Fertility

Moose are fertility junkies. They can only live under highly fertile conditions, on young soils, in juvenile ecosystems. The deep, soft soils of the Temperate Zone of the Northern Hemisphere support the rapid summer growth of tender, nutrient-rich plants. These soils are the product of the northern continental glaciations of the most recent ice ages. Glaciers grind rocks into a fine powder, which is called silt if it is carried by water and loess if it is carried by wind. The ground-up rock flour is exceptionally fertile, and the more rock types that are included in the rock flour, the more fertile it is. The soft, fertile soils of the northern Temperate Zone do not exist, indeed never have existed, in the Tropics, which escaped the glacial pulses of the last two million years or so. The closest equivalents in the Tropics are soils formed from silt and plant debris deposited annually by flooding rivers. Often these silts are liberated by ice and snow high in the mountains where these rivers originate.

Moose consume massive amounts of minerals, the likes of which are simply not available on the old, leached-out land surfaces of much of the Southern Hemisphere. Moose obtain the minerals they need either by feeding on mineral-rich plants or by visiting mineral licks. Plants that grow on silt carried by flooding rivers from mountain glaciers contain high levels of minerals, as do plants that grow in the ashes of forest fires. Trees on the taiga are rich in minerals because their roots break down rocks just as glaciers do. As the trees grow, they take up minerals from the underlying rocks. Forest fires then release the minerals stored in the trees' woody tissues, and the shrubs and herbs that follow the forest fires quickly absorb the minerals concentrated in the ashes. Thus the plants that colonize exposed soil in the wake of forest fires provide moose with a ready source of minerals.

Moose bounce back and forth between two principle types of habitat, one permanent and one transient. Flooding rivers that penetrate the taiga, that annually fill potholes and lakes, that scour floodplains with ice floes, and that deposit fertile silt along waterways and deltas form the permanent habitat of moose. Annual floods and the scouring action of ice knock back tree growth and allow the growth of willows, dogwood, sedges, and broad-leaved herbs known as forbs—weed species all. Small, shallow lakes are filled with aquatic vegetation. This ecosystem is perpetually immature and is known as a "pulse stabilized" ecosystem because its stability is a prod-

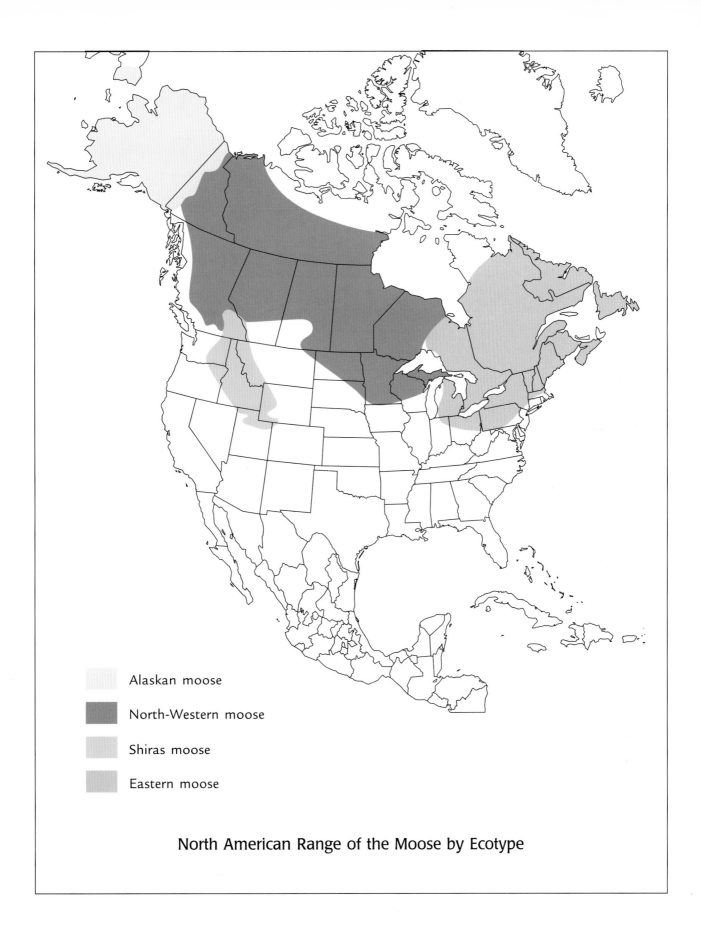

Alaskan moose

North-Western moose

Shiras moose

Eastern moose

North American Range of the Moose by Ecotype

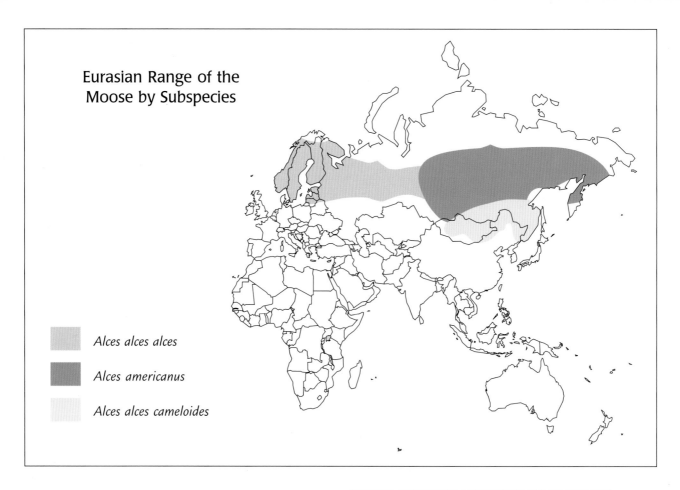

Eurasian Range of the Moose by Subspecies

Alces alces alces

Alces americanus

Alces alces cameloides

uct of annual pulses of water, scouring by floods and ice, and deposits of fertile silt. Here moose will always find food of high quality; however, the riparian and delta ecosystems are not extensive compared with the vast boreal forests that surround them.

Fires in boreal forests create the second type of high-quality habitat for moose. Forest fires are set by lightning. Most lightning strikes are in wet forests and, except for the trees hit, the fires fail to burn and spread. If lightning hits during a dry, hot spell, however, the resulting fire can be huge. Thus over the evolutionary history of moose, the species has depended on small areas of refuge habitat formed by flooding rivers, but has exploited large areas of transient, high-quality burn habitat formed unpredictably in space and time.

In addition to these two principal types of habitat, moose exploit marginal habitats and small pockets of fertility. They are occasionally found in marginal habitats such as the old-growth forests of western British Columbia. More often, they are found in pockets of fertility such as avalanche slopes in mountainous regions where the vegetation has

FACING PAGE: A cow feeds in a small pond in Alaska.

OVERLEAF: The Jackson Hole valley of Wyoming winters many moose. Moose are attracted to areas of low, hard snow. They are creatures enslaved to the law of least effort—as are we. For wintering moose, the energy saved by avoiding deep snow is significant. Moreover— and this may be more important—secure footing is vital for a moose defending itself. When danger threatens, moose choose hard, flat ground where they can flail and kick with front and hind legs in all directions. This is how moose defend themselves against wolves.

44

been returned to an earlier, more nutritious stage of its cycle, or in lush valleys where beavers form their ponds. Some beaver valleys silt in over millennia, burying old ponds and forming deep, rich soils that allow willows, aspen, and poplars to thrive.

Moose Staples

The most nutritious food for moose are the young leaves of the willow. These contain high concentrations of protein, calcium, and phosphate—the primary components of the apatite crystals that form bones. Adult moose need to restore their porous skeletons after winter, as bone is dissolved for metabolic purposes in times of nutrient shortage. In addition to adding bone mass to its skeleton, a large bull moose will grow 40 to 55 pounds (18–25 kg) of antler mass in some 140 days. This is about the same bone mass as is grown by a large calf by fall, or by a yearling moose weighing 330 to 440 pounds (150–200 kg). The bull's skeleton reaches its highest density in early fall, when solid bone is required to withstand the strain of fighting during the rutting season. Cow moose do not grow antlers, but they need to restore skeletons depleted of bone mass by pregnancy and lactation.

There are great seasonal variations in the food habits of moose. In spring before the willows put out their slender, shiny leaves, moose eat the catkins. In summer, when the metabolic effort of moose requires them to consume huge amounts of soft, nutrient-rich plant tissue, they strip the leaves off new willow shoots. They supplement their diet of willow leaves with the flora of alpine meadows and old burns, and with aquatic plants found in shallow lakes. In summer, feeding periods are short, because moose can strip the foliage from long twigs or bite off the flowering parts of tall annuals in large mouthfuls. They do not snip off grasses or aquatic sedges when they eat them, but rather pull them out, exposing the tender growing parts. This ensures the moose extract the maximum nutritional value from the plants they eat. In winter, moose are not actively growing and their metabolic requirements remain at maintenance levels so food intake is low. Woody browse is the mainstay of their diet at this time of year, and browsing moose clip off the annual woody shoots of willows. These young twigs have a relatively

ABOVE: Moose sign. In fall, winter, and early spring, moose feces are pelleted; in summer, when moose feed extensively on green foliage, their feces resemble the pies dropped by cattle.

FACING PAGE: Sign of a moose's passing. Bulls horn small conifers such as these white spruce, setting back the trees' growth or even killing them.

thick bark and little wood, which makes them more nutritious than older twigs that contain less bark and more wood. The collection of twigs, snipped off one by one, is a lengthy process and consequently feeding in the winter takes a long time.

Although moose favor deciduous shrubs and trees for food, and regionally exploit aquatic vegetation, they may also consume large amounts of coniferous browse. In the eastern parts of North America the preferred species is the balsam fir; in the West it is Douglas and alpine firs. Such conifers may be important winter food, and moose may linger high in the mountains feeding on low alpine firs, until snow conditions force them down to lower elevations. In Scandinavia, moose feeding on conifers may inflict considerable damage on commercial pine plantations, killing or stunting the trees. Moose also damage conifers by horning them with their antlers, debarking the trunks and ripping off branches.

As a foliage feeder and browser, the moose would have benefited from a long neck, like a giraffe; however, head-to-head wrestling with locked antlers—the style of fighting adopted by moose—requires a short neck. Despite their short necks, moose can reach far up into trees and shrubs, and a short, muscular neck

comes in handy when breaking off stems to get at high-growing twigs. If they need to, moose can reach tender early sedges by kneeling down.

Making the Most of Food

The moose is a concentrate feeder, that is a species that feeds on plants that are low in fiber and high in nutrients. The lack of fiber means that these plants are relatively easy to digest. Some of the plants that moose eat are highly toxic. Plants defend themselves against being eaten by various means, but the most common defense is to deposit toxic compounds into their leaves and bark. The richer a plant is in nutrients, and the more likely it is to be eaten by a herbivore, the more toxic it is, and the more toxic the parts readily available to herbivores. Consequently, leaves growing high in a tree are less toxic than those at the bottom, which is one reason deer and moose love to feed on the tops of fallen trees.

To deal with toxins, the moose has an exceptionally large liver that helps to metabolize secondary plant compounds (one reason moose liver tastes bitter). Since moose feed on plants that are low in fiber, they have relatively small rumens—the fermentation chamber for the vegetation they ingest. The rumen is an expansion of the gullet before the stomach. Anaerobic bacteria in the rumen digest the cellulose in the plant fibers. The body of the moose does not run on glucose, as the human body does, but on fatty acids, and over half of all digestible energy in the cellulose may be liberated as volatile fatty acids in the rumen. These fatty acids are then absorbed directly into the bloodstream. What little glucose the moose liberates during digestion is apparently slated to fuel the brain.

The rumen of the moose is its own closed ecosystem and the bacteria that live there are, in turn,

A bull in Elk Island National Park, Alberta, Canada, in October. In this fenced park, mature moose and bull elk carry small antlers, while bison feature reduced hair coats. The problem appears to be competition for adequate summer forage. At this time, antlers and hair coats grow and high-quality forage is essential. Summer forage turns toxic and fibrous, but the fence prevents the moose from moving to river valleys or mountains where summer forage is better.

fed on by a series of protozoan predators, which are a normal part of the rumen flora. In addition to digesting the cellulose in the plant fibers, the bacteria in the rumen, along with the protozoa that feed on them, synthesize a variety of diverse organic molecules, including many vitamins. These are liberated when the bacteria and protozoa pass into the true stomach of the moose—along with the fermenting rumen content—and are digested there by stomach enzymes.

After the initial fermentation process, the remaining coarse content of the rumen is returned to the mouth for rechewing or rumination. By this time, bacterial action has broken down the plant fibers and rechewing them—and resoaking them in saliva that contains urea—enhances the digestion of cellulose by the bacteria. Urea is formed from digested protein within the moose and it contains high levels of nitrogen. Humans excrete urea in their urine. Rumi-

ABOVE: Moose feeding in the Pelican Creek meadows in Yellowstone National Park. Do not expect to see moose here today. The willows that were found here once have disappeared with increasing use of the area by bison and elk. Willows are a major food source for moose, winter or summer.

FACING PAGE: Willows are the staff of life of moose. In winter, moose prefer to feed on annual willow twigs. These are encased in a nutritious but poisonous bark, which moose are able to utilize—thanks to their ability to detoxify secondary plant compounds.

nants, moose included, recycle urea and use it to increase the amount of nitrogen available for the bacteria in the rumen. The bacteria use nitrogen to synthesize protein. Since plant food is frequently low in nitrogen, soaking plant fibers in urea is a useful mechanism to increase the food value of the plant matter consumed. Once the living content of the rumen enters the stomach, hydrochloric acid secreted by the stomach walls dissolves the abundant protozoa and bacteria, liberating the protein of these unicellular organisms for digestion by the moose. Thus the bacteria and protozoa in the rumen serve not only to digest cellulose and to detoxify some of the many toxic compounds in the plants moose eat, but also to provide valuable protein to the moose.

Pre-fermenting plant food, and exploiting nutritionally the ferment and the fermenters, allows the moose and other ruminants to live on relatively less food than herbivores such as horses, elephants, and rhinos require to survive. These large browsers digest plant matter as it enters the true stomach without the benefit of a fermenting vat along the way. To

ABOVE: A bull beds down in Wyoming's Grand Teton National Park. Loose, fluffy snow is a favorite bedding medium that gives thermal protection to moose. In addition, moose frequently scoop up snow in place of drinking water.

FACING PAGE: Cow moose browsing on a Douglas fir in April. Moose can reach branches about eight feet (2.4 m) above ground. Some conifers such as firs are favored food, while others like spruce and pine are not. This cow is still in full winter coat.

get any nutritive value out of fibrous plants, a horse must thoroughly grind the food it ingests. Consequently, its teeth are huge, filling almost the entire skull. The teeth of moose, by comparison, are much more modest in size, as predigestion by bacteria reduces the resistance of the plant fibers to chewing, and browse and foliage are less abrasive to teeth than dust-covered grasses.

Although the horse gets far less nutrition from each mouthful of vegetation compared with the

54

ABOVE: A prime bull moose stands amid sagebrush. His distended belly indicates a moose long after the rut, one that has been feeding heavily and recovering body condition. Bulls after the rut are emaciated, having used up all fat deposits chasing females and fighting rivals. Good range in late fall and early winter, however, allows bull to regain fat for the hard winter ahead.

FACING PAGE: Moose in winter often search out alluvial flats along flooding creeks and rivers, be it in Alaska, Canada, or in Wyoming, as is the case here. Growing on the floodplains are favorite browse species such as willow, red osier dogwood, birch, and poplar. Annual floods bring fertile silt from the mountains, while ice scouring and wave action set back ecological succession, keeping floodplains perpetually young, fertile, and productive.

moose, in one respect its digestive system is more efficient. In times of poor forage, a horse can clear its gut more rapidly than a moose can clear its rumen. Thus the horse can increase the throughput of food but the moose cannot. Even though the horse digests less of the poor-quality food, by increasing its rate of feeding, it can keep up a high rate of nutrient flow across the gut wall into its body. The moose cannot increase its rate of feeding to compensate for poor-quality forage. When the food supply is fibrous and low in protein, the rumen of the moose becomes filled with coarse plant fibers, and the animal may starve to death. Thus a horse can manage on forage that would not allow a moose to thrive.

The mobile, highly sensitive muzzle of the moose appears to be specialized for effective underwater feeding. Indeed, moose are not only able to feed standing in shallow water, but they may swim and dive for aquatic vegetation. Although other species of deer occasionally feed on aquatic weeds, moose are unique in routinely seeking out this food source. These aquatic plants appear to aid moose in their mineral nutrition, as boreal forest plants, growing on acidic soil, are notoriously short of sodium. In the absence of mineral licks, aquatic plants are a source of sodium, which is an essential mineral in body metabolism. In western North America, moose appear to get the sodium they require from mineral licks and are rarely seen feeding on aquatic vegetation. In winter, moose are also attracted to highways that are salted to reduce icing in the interests of automobile safety, which can lead to accidents that are fatal to both the occupants of the car and to the moose.

Where possible, moose visit mineral licks, occasionally making long excursions to particularly rich and exposed mineral deposits. The visits of moose to mineral licks and springs correlate fairly closely with the shedding of their old coat and the growing of the new one, with antler growth in bulls, with milk production in cows, and with the restoration of the body after the depredations of winter. That is, the metabolic salts available in mineral licks are required in early summer when the body is most metabolically active. The bacteria in the rumen convert minerals into bacterial protoplasm. Since moose digest the bacteria that ferment their food, they can use the protein from the bacterial protoplasm to fuel periods of rapid growth. Moose often linger at mineral licks for a day or two before returning to their summer ranges.

Moose not only like mineral licks and springs, but also hot springs, where they may soak in the steaming water—obviously enjoying the experience, much as we do. The heavily browsed vegetation about such hot pools indicates how much moose enjoy these springs. They stay until the need for food finally wins out and they move off to distant feeding grounds.

The Finishing Touches

Nutrition alone does not ensure proper growth. Bones do not grow without appropriate exercise, nor do muscles, blood vessels, and nerves. This adaptive need expresses itself as play. Young, growing moose and also adult moose during the season when their bodies are growing love to play. Moose are most active on cool days or in the cool morning or evening hours.

Adult bulls, on vacation from the serious occupation of breeding during the short rutting season, are sociable in spring and early summer. They gather in small groups, and it is within these groups that they may play exuberantly. Occasionally a barren cow joins them. The pregnant cows, however, are terribly serious about life: they avoid other moose or chase them off, they barely tolerate their calves from the previous year, and they stay hidden in forest and shrubbery much of the time. Not so bulls and barren cows. They readily accept open spaces, mainly seasonally flooded sedge meadows, where they feed, rest—and play.

A cow feeds on aquatic sedges, uprooting them and ingesting the bulbous root and all. The moose's muzzle is a complex, highly innervated feeding organ that lets moose maximize the quality of food they extract from plants. It also allows moose to feed effectively underwater, something no other deer has mastered as well. Many species of large concentrate and foliage feeders have evolved specialized nasal organs—such as tapirs, elephants, and many extinct forms—to select and extract the most nutritious portion of the foliage.

Moose and water have a long association, as moose fossils are notoriously preserved in aquatic deposits. Moose are also excellent swimmers that do not shun swimming out into the ocean—where they have been seen attacked and devoured by killer whales.

ABOVE: After dunking its head under water in search of food, a cow lowers it ears to allow water to run out. Therefore, the ears-low expression is not a threat, as often believed. Moose bring aquatic plants to the surface to masticate and swallow. They are concentrate feeders with a small rumen and rapid fermentation of food, and also have a huge liver to break down toxic secondary plant compounds. Moose achieve their highest body growth on a diverse rather than a monotonous diet. The food intake of moose in summer is prodigious, for moose grow and fatten in this short season.

Half a dozen bull moose may run as a group, chase one another, perform mock attacks, or hit puddles with their front hooves and then spin around and kick at the puddles so that sheets of water fly high into the air. In the running games the bulls may trot rapidly one after the other, lifting the legs high and tucking in their chins, like horses in dressage. A swollen creek in their path is no obstacle. One after the other the bulls jump up and dive in. Their legs are extended when their bellies hit the water with a huge splash. They submerge entirely, but quickly surface and—still trotting with legs lifted high and chins tucked in—rush from the creek across the meadow. Moose love to play in water and may splash exuberantly in the waves of the ocean, attacking each breaker as it rolls in.

Although they often play together when they congregate in the spring, moose do not need company to play. Single bulls and cows may run about on their own and attack puddles, striking at these with the front legs after rearing up. During the attack they assume the defensive threat so characteristic of moose, as if the puddle were a wolf, a bear, or another moose. Rarely, a moose may play with a floating object, such as a piece of wood, while standing belly deep in water. Manipulating objects with its mouth is part of the feeding behavior of a moose, as it uses its sensitive muzzle to manipulate twigs prior to biting them off. It is as if the moose were testing to see how pliable the twigs are, rejecting the dead, dry ones in favor of tender, living shoots. Once a twig is clipped off between the incisor teeth in the lower jaw and the horny plate in the upper jaw, the moose turns the twig around and ingests it base first.

For moose watchers, annual twigs clipped off willow bushes, red osier dogwood, and other tree and shrub species are sure signs of the presence of moose. A moose may also break branches up to an inch (2.54 cm) thick in order to reach the annual twigs. It does this by grasping a branch with its mouth and rotating its head so that the branch breaks. Other telltale signs of the passing of moose are tooth scars on aspen trees where moose have scraped off bark in the winter. The light wood exposed by the barking is visible a long way off.

Forage intake is high in spring and summer when moose grow, lay down fat, lactate, and replace

The bulls are back together. The competition of the rut is past and the bulls are, once again, on vacation until next fall. Note their black noses, which identify them as bulls after they shed their antlers. These are old males from Wyoming. In dense populations, bulls join with others, but tend to segregate by age—young with young, old with old.

their coats, and low in winter when they do not. Even though they spend a long time feeding in the winter, their intake is not sufficient to meet daily demands and needs to be subsidized by breaking down their stores of fat. This process liberates not only energy, but also the vitamins stored in the body fat. Despite their desperate need for food in winter, moose cannot risk going wherever there is good browse. They have to be on guard for predators, wolves in particular. Moose feed only where it is secure. Even then, a wolf howl announcing the arrival of a pack will cause moose to depart from their feeding grounds in a hurry. A large burn filled with peacefully browsing moose can be emptied in half an hour as moose quickly leave before the wolves arrive.

Security

When I got my first job as a biologist in British Columbia in 1959, I was instructed to observe moose. One of my tasks was to find out what they fed on. This was often a puzzle, especially when the moose buried its nose deep in the high herb carpet of a wet subalpine meadow and failed to raise its head. Tall associations of alpine herbs were favorite feeding sites, a welcome change in menu from willow leaves, fireweeds, or pondweeds. Yet, just what did the moose pick? A spotting scope, no matter how good, was little help. At long distances, wavy hot summer air distorts the image, making exact observation difficult. Nor is the spotting scope much help when the moose muzzle is obscured by vegetation.

Walking up to the moose to observe it more closely might work with moose in a national park that are habituated to people, but it did not work with the wild moose I was studying in central British Columbia. Worse, moose that have been spooked won't return to an observation area—although moose change feeding locality from day to day, they still eventually return to where they were observed earlier—consequently, it is important that they remain unaware of one's presence. That means silently exploring places where breezes are not likely to signal one's presence to the moose's sensitive nose.

A bull hides deep within a stand of trees, spying on interlopers to its domain.

How about stalking close? I quickly discovered that the rustling noises made by my clothing were a problem. Shedding shoes and dress, however, made all those extra noises disappear. It was bearable in the hot sun as long as there were few mosquitoes. Bare feet are marvelously silent when walking on a mat of herbs, mosses, decaying wood, roots, and branches. As my feet felt the way, I kept an eye on the moose and silently parted branches with my hands. I made my way forward step by silent step. When a moose looked up, I froze until it finished glancing about, then resumed my silent advance. Using this method, I got very close to moose. I did not push my luck, but the moose seemed oblivious to my presence even when I was as close as five paces. Getting closer than that I judged not to be too healthy. All the wild moose I got close to were busy tearing the unopened flowers of alpine herbs and chewing them noisily, drowning out any small sounds I might make.

The best moose to stalk and observe were young bulls, because they were distinctly less careful than old bulls or cows with calves. Cows with calves are potentially dangerous and I usually gave them a wide berth. One old bull that limped had apparently had an encounter with hunters. He paid close attention to unusual sounds and if he heard any he left at once. While young bulls ignored the sound of my hatchet as I chopped through a dry spruce branch that I needed to start a fire, the old bull did not, even though he was at least eight hundred paces away. Once I surprised him from about one hundred paces off when I rounded a small hill. He immediately dove from sight into an old creek bed. I rushed forward, expecting to see him leave in the direction he had taken. No moose. I turned around and saw him rounding the hill behind me, leaving in the direction from which I had arrived. He had quickly run a circle around me in cover I thought would not hide a moose. I was to learn in many years of fieldwork that this is a common tactic for moose intent on shaking a pursuer.

Escape Strategies

To a deer security is everything. The same is true for moose. Deer escape predators either by jumping over obstacles and hiding in cover, or by running with speed and endurance across open plains to lose themselves in the vastness of space. The white-tailed deer and roe deer exemplify the former style; the caribou exemplifies the latter. Jumpers are called "saltors" and runners are called "cursors." Their different body plans fit their respective modes of escape.

Saltors elude predators by choosing escape routes strewn with obstacles, and then hiding in cover. They are forest dwellers who do not stray far from protective vegetation, and they tire quickly. And little wonder: jumping over obstacles uses up thirteen times as much energy as traversing level ground. Cursors escape predators by outrunning them. They have great endurance and run with great economy of motion, keeping their bodies dead level or nearly so. Cursors have short legs when they live on level terrain with little vegetation or snow depth; they have long legs where the terrain requires the skilled placement of feet around obstacles. An example of the former is the oryx, which lives in semidesert regions of Africa, and an example of the latter is the pronghorn, which lives on the Great Plains of North America.

Saltors and cursors are the two extremes in running adaptation. The moose combines elements of both: it has great endurance and can clear predator-shedding obstacles with ease. The moose has long legs for its body size. It can trot rapidly and at little cost in energy over obstacles its predators can clear only at great cost. In Sweden, a trotting moose was paced at 38 miles per hour (60 km/h) over obstructed terrain—not much slower than a white-tailed deer galloping full speed over unobstructed ground. As the moose trots, it keeps its body dead level, floating elegantly over windfalls, hummocks, and bushes. Pursuing wolves must either jump over or run around each obstacle. Every inch of body lift adds rapidly to the predator's fatigue, while dodging obstacles and preparing for jumps slows them down. The specialized trot of the moose thus exploits its superiority in body size and leg length over would-be predators.

It is clear that, given its escape strategy, large body size and long legs are vital to a moose's survival. Small moose cannot trot over high enough obstacles to tire out predators rapidly. Consequently, one does not expect to find small moose except where pursu-

Wolves and moose go together. Both are East Siberian in origin, which means that they coexisted throughout the Ice Ages, and their ancestors lived side by side before that. Yet moose are not a favorite prey of wolves, because moose are dangerous to wolves—as autopsies on numerous wolves that preyed on moose have revealed. If they have a choice, wolves much prefer deer, caribou, or elk. After all, moose not only strike with deadly precision with their front hooves, but also lash out with their hind legs. Such kicks are accurate and bone-crushingly powerful.

Track Comparison of Moose with other Adult North American *Cervidae*

Whitetail deer (*Odocoileus virginianus*) and **Mule deer** (*Odocoileus hemionus*)
Length: Approximately 3 inches 7½ cm)
Distance between tracks: 20 inches (50 cm)

Caribou (*Rangifer caribou*)
Length: Approximately 4 inches (10 cm) without dew claws
Distance between tracks: 20–40 inches (50–100 cm)

Elk (*Cervus canadensis*)
Length: Approximately 4½ inches (11¼ cm)
Distance between tracks: 24–36 inches (60–90 cm)

Moose (*Alces alces*)
Length: Approximately 7 inches (17½ cm)
Distance between tracks: 24–60 inches (60–150 cm)

ing predators are absent—an unlikely situation. Body size is critical in minimizing predation; thus moose born in years of poor body growth are more likely to fall prey to wolves than moose from years of good body growth. Since obstacles two to three feet (60–90 cm) in height are essential to the security of moose, it is little wonder that they rarely venture into unobstructed terrain. They spend most of their time partly hidden by shrubs, tall sedges, or water. Only when they step out onto short grass or a frozen lake can one appreciate just how long legged they are. Another reason one rarely sees moose in the open is that they must not only choose habitats with plenty of obstacles, but also know exactly where these obstacles are located. Thus it is in their best interests to stick close to a familiar home range centered on suitable escape terrain.

Moose, like all species of deer, have more than one defensive strategy. Not only can they trot rapidly for long distances over obstructed terrain, they can also hide masterfully, swim well, and place themselves strategically to smell, hear, or see danger. Un-

ABOVE: On a dry road in Yellowstone National Park surrounded by deep, hard snow in early spring, a moose attacks a car that came too close. A hard, dry surface is escape terrain that moose are most unlikely to give up readily; on such ground moose can pivot most readily and strike out in any direction. This bull rose on his hind legs and pummeled the car from the hood to the trunk as it went by.

FACING PAGE: Moose are a winter deer, different from caribou in detail but not in principle. A snow blanket of modest depth does not hinder moose, but rather allows them to shed pursuing predators. They can glide with little body lift over snow that wolves can only master with expensive bounding. Frozen, snow-covered lakes are an escape terrain for moose that allows for secure footing, and thus for an excellent defense against encroaching wolves. In deep, hard snow, however, moose plow a network of trails—the famous moose yards. Hard snow crusts favor wolves rather than moose.

der certain circumstances, they may also confront and attack large predators.

Moose have excellent senses and may detect danger at great distances and with precision. Old bulls are particularly good at distancing themselves from potential danger. One late December day, after I had crested a ridge on snowshoes, I saw an old bull across the valley on a burn. He was about a mile (1.6 km) away, yet he stood facing toward me, fully alert. He turned with head held high, laid back his antlers, and, at a brisk trot, diagonally ascended a steep mountain. On he climbed, until he was but a dot, going ever higher over snow-covered windfalls. Then he branched off into a small patch of open fir forest that had been missed by the forest fire. Here I saw him turn around and immediately lie down facing the way he had come. I was using an excellent spotting scope—with mere binoculars he would have been too far away to observe by then.

This bull used several escape strategies common to the moose. First he detected me from far away. We do not have precise data on vision in moose, but like all deer, they probably have limited color vision. Close observations indicate that moose are most sensitive to the movement patterns of distant objects, and in open areas they flee from danger detected in

---

The dominance display of the bull. One of the most common and important behaviors of dominant males is to display their status to rivals, as well as mates. In the deer family, this is often done by a combination of body and antler display in which unusual movements, and prominent body parts attract the onlooker's attention. Bull moose display by approaching rivals slowly and deliberately at a tangent—not directly—while tipping their antlers very noticeably from side to side with each step. The ears are laid back and the approaching bull vocalizes a loud "oou-ch"—almost a moan—with each alternate step. The displaying bull circles in this manner around the rival, who, if of comparable size, is likely to reply in kind. Dominance displays precede fights by matched males, but, used by large bulls, may also initiate sparring. In interactions between matched bulls, dominance displays are interrupted by vigorous horning of shrubs and small trees. The dominance display of the moose resembles that of American deer. It even includes the dragging of hooves over the ground, as can be seen when an early snowfall covers the rutting grounds of moose.

ABOVE: Moose periodically scan for danger. They have excellent hearing and a superlative sense of smell.

RIGHT: These bull moose were surprised by wolves hunting willow ptarmigan in Denali National Park, Alaska. Here moose have the upper hand. They stand in knee-high shrubs where moose, but not wolves, can run at maximum speed. The long legs and specialized gait of moose allow them to glide over low obstacles while wolves and grizzly bears falter.

the distance. The old bull moose I was following distanced himself from me across difficult terrain. Snow-covered old burns in the wet belt of central British Columbia are difficult to traverse due to a myriad of tall, wind-felled trees. After traveling nearly a mile, the bull swung right angle with the gentle breeze and moved about 150 paces away from the direction of his travel. He then lay down behind a fallen log watching his tracks, while the breeze blew squarely toward him. That moose was safe from hunters or predators. Anyone approaching would have been seen, heard, and smelled by the old bull resting deep in the loose snow.

The sensitivity of old moose notwithstanding, some weather factors do allow a careful human to closely approach moose. When there is deep, loose snow on the ground—particularly when masses of snowflakes are gently falling; when the wind rustles branches and leaves; or when the rain pelts down, softening dry leaves while splashing on tree trunks, leaves, and water surfaces, the fine senses of the moose are dulled. Native hunters in North America knew this well. When they located a desirable moose, they would wait until a wind blew up and then move in for the kill. Once, on an overcast November day when masses of snowflakes descended and the ground was covered by a foot (30 cm) of soft snow, I followed the tracks of three moose until they rose suddenly, the closest about six paces away. A cow then turned towards me, hackles up, and I was lucky that by shouting and quickly stepping backwards I convinced her not to attack. In the meantime the other two cows rose and, hackles raised, slowly moved off. The gentle sound of falling snowflakes, plus the soft snow underfoot, had dramatically obscured the senses of these three moose.

Although humans have excellent eyesight and adequate hearing compared with other large mammals, our ability to decipher smells is underdeveloped. By observing dogs we can deduce what goes on in the world of smell. In much of Europe, moose are hunted with elkhounds. The experience of hunters who use dogs to track moose sheds some light on the mysterious subject of scent.

Moose, which have just a few small scent glands, minimize the scent they leave behind them. They mark themselves extensively with strong-smelling

Roused from her bed while in cover, a cow moose examines the disturbance prior to fleeing, its ears up. When surprised at close quarters, moose either dash off or attack. However, the latter is—fortunately for people—a rare event. When a moose turns its ears forward and lowers them, that is a threat signal. The threatening cow's elevated head indicates curiosity.

urine only during the rut; however, some moose do urinate on their hind legs when they are disturbed, leaving spots of urine in the snow as they run away. It is not clear why they do this. Perhaps to make pursuing wolves sniff each spot of urine, thus delaying them and allowing the moose a better chance of escape. Moose escape detection by wolves and hunting dogs by staying downwind of their own tracks, and they confuse their pursuers by zigzagging across their own tracks. They also minimize their scent trails by walking in water. In still, wet weather moose are difficult to scent. In windy weather, when their scent might be picked up by predators, they are skittish and exceptionally alert.

Hunters who track moose with dogs report that moose behave differently depending on how many are in an area. Where moose are few, they tend to run long distances and may fail to come to bay. Where densities are high, moose are more likely to stand their ground and confront the dogs. Why this is so is puzzling. As expected, cow moose with calves are more likely to face down dogs. Groups of moose are more likely to run than single moose, and if one moose confronts a dog, the other moose are likely to sneak away. In general, European moose are quite reluctant to face hunting dogs, much as North American moose are reluctant to face down wolves. There are particular circumstances, however, under which moose will stand their ground and attack.

Moose on the Attack

If a moose is suddenly confronted by a predator at short range, it is likely to stand its ground. A moose on the attack quickly rears up on its hind legs and strikes out with its front legs. The hooves of moose are large and their leg bones are dense and heavy. A blow from the legs of a moose can kill a wolf, a human, or even a bear. Healed skull fractures and broken ribs observed in Alaskan wolves attest to the force of these blows. A moose can also whirl around and strike out with surprising rapidity and unerring accuracy with one or both of its extremely long hind legs. A friend of mine was once straddling an eight-foot-high (2.5-m) squeeze shoot when the antlerless bull trapped inside suddenly lashed out with both hind legs. He caught my friend squarely between the legs, hurling him from his lofty perch. This tactic is effective because of the element of surprise. Beware a moose raising a hind leg slightly off the ground, as it is likely getting ready to kick.

In the days of flint, black powder, and lead shot, Siberian hunters feared moose more than they feared big brown bears. A bear can be killed with a lance, particularly if dogs distract it, or—if worse comes to worst—with a large knife. A wounded moose turning on its tormentors cannot be readily speared or knifed, and the low power of a small-caliber, black-powder gun with soft, ballistically inefficient lead bullets, is not likely to stop a charging moose. The skull of the moose is solid and covered by a tough skin about half an inch (1.25 cm) thick. The neck of a bull moose in rut is covered by skin about an inch (2.54 cm) thick. This tough elastic hide can absorb enough energy from a high-powered rifle to make shots to the neck futile. A round lead ball fired from a black-powder gun would quickly flatten after hitting the tough skin; a mere knife would slide off. The shoulder blade of a big bull is so tough that it can turn and even stop heavy bullets fired from modern high-performance rifles. Moreover, mortally wounded moose can still put up a stiff fight before expiring. An attacking moose would be difficult to kill from the front with primitive weapons.

Moose have a sophisticated security system that insures that wolves must work hard for every bite of moose meat. Wolves prefer to hunt almost any prey

---

Moose and forest fires go together. Coniferous climax forests removed by fire give way to early successional stages of herbaceous plants and deciduous shrubs and trees. Fires release nutrients held captive in wood. These burns form prime moose habitat. In fact, much of moose biology is designed to capitalize on rather sudden expanses of virgin moose range, which only forest fires can create. However, not all fires create usable moose habitat. In some areas wildfires give rise to dense pine stands, which are not suitable for moose. In this photograph we see a bull moose a year and a half after the famous Yellowstone wildfire of fall of 1988. This is not yet good moose range, but clearly will be soon. Before the wildfire this area wintered bull elk. They came, attempted to winter, and died. Now moose and elk are again using this very same burn.

Cow moose produce about 440 pounds (200 kg) of milk during a four- to five-month period. Moose milk is much richer in solids than that of domestic cattle, which aids the calf in its exceptionally rapid growth. Security in moose depends on their ability to cross obstacles effortlessly, and defend themselves against predators. Both depend on calves reaching large body size. Calves may exceed 260 to 440 pounds (120–200 kg) in fall, and yet depend on their mothers to defend them against wolves in winter.

A healthy moose calf in Denali National Park, Alaska. Moose calves call loudly and plaintively when in distress, a sound that can quickly bring mother—or attentive bears and wolves—to the scene. Because the survival of moose calves depends on mother's undoubted propensity for violence, calves have a most expressive "help me" call. Lone calves are unlikely to survive wolf predation. They depend on their big mothers for protection.

other than moose, because moose are dangerous when confronted and employ many sophisticated means of thwarting predators. When the snow blanket is low and soft and moose can move around relatively easily, they tend to leave an area when wolves arrive. I vividly remember one cold day in January when I was observing about a dozen bull moose scattered across a burn in a small valley. They were feeding and resting, a picture of quiet contentment. Then the deep howl of a wolf rang out across the valley. All the bulls were on their feet at once. They looked down the valley. Then one by one they turned and left. Within twenty minutes the valley was free of moose.

Wolves closely comb any area occupied by moose. From one day to the next a valley used by moose may be crisscrossed with wolf tracks, so that one finds a track every twenty paces or less. No moose can escape this close scrutiny undetected.

Wolves or no wolves, moose cannot readily leave an area in late winter when the snow is deep. Later still, from late March onward, the deep snow develops a hard, icy surface layer called a sun crust. This happens when daytime temperatures rise and the sun shines on the snow. The surface of the snow softens during the day and then freezes rock hard during the night. Although such crusts are great for snowshoeing, they handicap moose. Moose caught trying to escape through deep, crusted snow flounder pitifully and can neither run away nor defend themselves. In late winter, therefore, moose stay close to areas of low snow and good footing, such as frozen ponds or windswept hilltops. When I approached moose in such locations, instead of running away, they would move to a place with good footing and then turn to face me menacingly. Calves hid behind their mothers. Occasionally, a moose would back into a conifer, as if trying to protect its rear. Clearly, the moose is looking for a place where it can use its powerful legs, striking at whoever dares to come close—in most cases moose assume this position to threaten wolves.

This explains why late winter is one time moose are particularly likely to stand up to predators. It is then that the snow pack is at its highest and hardest, which severely handicaps the mobility of moose. In addition, by mid- to late winter, moose are often on their own. Moose space themselves out because this makes it easier to find food. Whereas a lone moose may find enough to eat while mired in deep snow, a group of moose would quickly consume all the nearby food. Spreading out is adaptive as it conserves precious food supplies; however, it leaves each moose on its own when wolves come to visit. Food shortages and deep snow change the disposition of moose from flight and tolerance to aggression.

Although moose can be dangerous, they clearly signal their intent. A moose shifting weight to one hind leg is likely to lash out backwards with the other. A moose lowering its ears and head and raising the long hair on its neck and rump is likely to rush at an intruder. Although this is a defensive threat, and the moose will likely only strike the ground loudly with its front hooves, it may occasionally attack and claim a victim. When moose cannot move around easily to find food, they must do all they can to conserve energy. Thus, where possible, they stick to well-worn trails, and instead of running away from potential danger, they choose to stay put. They may move onto roads, refusing to budge or attacking people. On railway tracks surrounded by deep snow, they often become victims of trains. Moose in these conditions should never be approached. Leave them to amble off in their own time. Give them lots of space, do not approach them, and never underestimate a moose.

Like many large mammals that confront predators, moose are dark in color. From a wolf's eye view, the moose is black. It is much lighter on its back, but wolves do not see the back when confronting moose. Just why predators should associate the color black with danger remains to be discovered. A moose threatening to attack takes on the appearance of a huge, vicious dog. It adopts the defensive behavior of the wolf and does not look much like a deer at all. The long hairs on its neck, withers, and croup rise. It

In deep snow, moose tend to forage in shady conifer forests where the snow is relatively low and, shaded from the sun, remains soft. This cow has living proof of this on her face. She has been foraging below the snow blanket for herbs, but also evergreen shrubs such as false box and Oregon grape.

ABOVE: The calf sticks closely to its mother and follows her lead in most activities.

FACING PAGE: The calf's survival depends on its protective
mother. The cow may stand guard over its sleeping calf.
Calves do not hide when danger threatens; rather, they run
to their large, capable mothers.

Deep, soft snow is not a great impediment to moose. They still move out to feed on willows in the open, and during resting, take advantage of the thermal properties of snow. Unlike mountain sheep, moose do not rest on compacted, icy snow, and do not rest in the same bed twice.

lowers its head to face attacking wolves at their level. It also lowers its ears and turns them forward. Then it bursts forward at its enemy.

A moose in danger may also emit a number of unusual sounds. When I first heard a moose roar, I was out on a trail on snowshoes. I tore the rifle from my shoulders, ready to defend myself, only to discover that the sound was made not by a grizzly awakening from hibernation somewhere under my feet, but by a young bull moose mired in snow some distance away. His warning roar carried loud and clear along the high mountain valley. A moose may also grind its teeth during a confrontation. Or, while bursting forward at the enemy, a moose may strike the ground loudly with its front hooves. It may also cock its hind leg to strike a blow backward at the enemy.

Wolves are capable but reluctant predators of

moose. Wolf packs test moose and do not attack those that show some spunk and face the pack. Wolves pursue moose that show little confidence and run away, usually the very young or the very old. Since moose have difficulty defending themselves against packs of wolves, they need to choose favorable ground when wolves attack. It is likely that moose that flee will eventually be forced to defend themselves on ground not of their own choosing. They may become mired in snow, they may fail to find a conifer with enough stout, low branches to offer protection from the rear, or they may be hampered by shrubbery when lashing out with their powerful legs. Whatever the reason, fleeing moose may soon be bitten severely by wolves. The wolves then allow them to weaken until they can be taken down with little risk.

In summer, moose approached by wolves may

run into shallow water. Here they turn and face the wolves, because in shallow water the long-legged moose retains better footing than the shorter-legged wolf. To flee into deep water, however, could be fatal. Deep water provides little protection for moose since wolves can attack and dismember prey while swimming. Where moose and wolves live, both the winter snows and the summer trails are often quite soft. Wolves, like caribou and reindeer, have evolved large feet, presumably so that they may have better footing on snow and soft soil. These large feet act as paddles when wolves swim. Wolves are fast and highly agile in the water, and do not hesitate to attack swimming prey. The swimming wolf, upon catching up to its prey, climbs partially onto the helpless victim and begins dismembering it right in the water.

Just as moose prefer shallow water to no water or deep water when confronting wolves, so they prefer a snow depth of about 20 inches (50 cm) to shallower or deeper snow. This may be because wolves are somewhat encumbered in 20 inches (50 cm) of snow, whereas moose lose essential maneuverability only in snow 30 inches (80 cm) or higher. Also, when the snow grows hard and crusty in the open, moose move into the shelter of coniferous forests, where the shadows of the dense canopy preclude sun crusts from forming.

Although moose are most often threatened by wolves, bears—both grizzly and black—also prey on moose. Experiments that transplanted grizzly bears out of Alaskan moose range resulted in increased survival rates for moose calves. Where bears are rare, such as in Scandinavia, the appearance of a bear causes noticeable disturbance to moose. Current research indicates that black bears are skilled at taking down prey at night. Just how they do this, however, remains to be discovered, as black bears are extremely secretive.

Occasional predators of moose, especially calves, are wolverine and lynx. A lynx cannot snap a moose calf's large neck, as it does a newborn caribou. Lynx likely attack as wolves do, biting and scratching calves and following them until they become weak from blood loss and infections.

The death of a moose brought down by a bear or wolf pack is neither swift nor merciful. The large size and tough hide of the moose prevent predators from opening big wounds that lead to rapid hemorrhaging. I once observed the aftermath of the death struggle of an old cow moose brought down by a grizzly. The grasses and forbs in the area had been trampled extensively and were liberally covered with blood and hair. Eventually the bear had opened up the rib cage, letting air into the pleural cavity. This prevented the lungs from expanding with each expansion of the rib cage. In short, the cow moose had suffocated.

Moose Hunt

Humans are also predators of moose. Moose were uncommon during glacial periods, and there is little evidence of humans hunting moose in the Ice Ages. Following the retreat of the continental ice masses and the conversion of periglacial steppe into fields of willows and dwarf birch or boreal forest, moose became common. They were clearly vital to aboriginal hunting cultures living in boreal forests. Cultures that depended on moose took pains to manage the welfare of this important food source. These people who depended on moose for meat, fat, leather, and bones discovered early that self-imposed restraint in killing moose was essential to tribal welfare. The same restraint is not evident where moose were occasional kills, or where most of the people's food came from plants or fat fish. The archeological record reveals that where native people lived primarily off plant food or fish, they hunted large mammals, excepting deer, virtually to extinction.

Humans make up in stamina what they lack in speed. They are also excellent trackers. In winter, with adequate snow on the ground, a well-conditioned man on snowshoes can run down and kill a moose. When I worked in the wilderness in winter and traveled long distances on snowshoes in low temperatures, I craved the rich fat of moose. After a long, hard day on the trail, the image of a moose steak with a wonderful ring of slightly yellow fat spurred me on through the night toward my cabin. The colder the weather, the greater that craving. The meat was good, but the fat was better, much better. I understood to the core of my bones why northern people cherish moose and why they need them as part of their life. I understood why they celebrate the kill of a fine, fat

moose cow in late winter, or a bull loaded with rich back fat and tender meat after the rest of a slothful summer.

I do not know how wolves eye such a delicacy, but I have lived "wild" enough to salivate at the memory of the wonderful feasts moose provided, and to cherish the memory of my hunting companions. Happiness was their laughter as we gutted and skinned moose; happiness was the smell of the meat roasting, suspended from a sharp stick beside the fire; happiness was the hot tea poured from sooty billy cans; happiness was carrying out heavy packs of moose meat over many miles of trail in their company. Though we came from the distant reaches of Eurasia and North America, while engaged in hunting—this most primeval, deeply emotional pursuit— we were blood brothers welded together by an affection and loyalty that mere words fail to describe.

ABOVE: Moose are excellent swimmers, as this young Wyoming moose proves.

FACING PAGE: A bull drinks from a pond in Maine.

LEFT: A cow-guarding bull threatens a persistent yearling bull, who ducks away in submission. A yearling bull avoiding a large bull may vocalize like a courted cow.

BELOW: Cows tend to frequent open shorelines and shallow water during the rut. In the western mountains, rutting moose may congregate at the timberline. Searching moose find one another by following these edges.

Chapter 4

Mating Games

Bull moose make the most of long summer days to fatten for the strenuous mating period ahead. Their body shape changes as their backs and upper haunches grow larger and larger, until their stubby tails become almost cone shaped and their bellies become distended. Native North Americans look upon such bulls with pleasure. Moose are best to eat when they are maximally fat in late August, when the long, thin pods of the maturing fireweeds have opened to release their seeds on parachutes of silky white fluff. By then the bulls have shed their old coats and grown glossy new ones. They are about to shed the velvet of their antlers so they can use them in sparring, fighting, and bragging, but for now they are comfortable and peaceful. They continue to feed avidly and follow much the same routine they have followed all summer.

As soon as the velvet comes off their antlers, the bulls are ready for some harmless sparring. These matches are true sporting engagements without loss of status to either participant.

The bulls feed at dawn, then rest for about an hour. Then they rise, feed for twenty to thirty minutes, and rest again. So it goes all day, until an appetite for roaming hits them at dusk and they move off to spend the next day elsewhere. A short feeding bout followed by a short nap is an efficient way to ferment the highly digestible food that bulls feed on in late summer. They pass the food through their rumens fairly rapidly and do not absorb all the water and nutrients from the digesta. Consequently, the summer droppings are soft and form patties not unlike those of domestic cows.

Mosquitoes, black flies, stable flies, horse flies, and deer flies do not seem to bother moose nearly as much as the heat. Using a spotting scope on a sunny day, one can see the glimmering of myriad mosquito wings on the bodies of moose. Unlike caribou in the same country, moose do not seek refuge from these bloodsuckers in lakes. No studies have yet quantified the impact of biting flies on moose; however, caribou may die from insect pest harassment. The moose I observed on open burns did not seem too bothered by the flies. They did, however, seek refuge from extreme heat, disrupting their rest periods on very hot days to lie down in the shallow water of a small sedge meadow. They did not go so far as to leave the open burn to seek out the shade of the dense alpine fir forest, as they do later during the rut. Fattening in early summer is a serious business and must not be disrupted.

Whereas bull moose are frequently observed in open areas, cows with calves spend more time hiding in the forest. Cows need to maximize security for their calves; bulls need to maximize food intake to grow the largest, most powerful bodies and antlers possible. They take their chances with predators in order to be in the best feeding areas. Provided the bulls survive, this maximizes their chances of dominating other bulls and of displacing other bulls from cows in the rutting season. Cows feed on whatever is available in their hiding areas. They can do this without compromising their ability to give birth to healthy calves, because cows must never maximize the birth size of their calves. A calf too large to pass through the birth canal would kill its mother. Cows must therefore optimize birth size: calves too small are not viable, but calves too large, will either kill their mothers or suffer organ damage as they are born. Bulls and cows therefore separate quite naturally, with bulls favoring habitats rich in food and cows favoring habitats that are secure.

The transition from fattening to rutting begins when the bulls stand for extended periods after feeding, as if reluctant to lie down and chew their cuds. The antlers are fully grown, and the velvet covering shows light spots. The body shape is almost a rectangle because of the massive deposition of fat on the croup. Occasionally two bulls meet and stay together for a day or two. The first restlessness is apparent. The first timid antler contact is made on bushes, a sign that the velvet will be shed from the antlers within days. As feeding declines, the potbellies of the bulls tighten noticeably.

Dominance Displays

Velvet shedding in old bulls commences in early September. Long strips of bloody velvet hang for a few days from the base of the bright, yellow-white antlers. Bulls thrash their antlers in bushes or rub them against the pliable stems of young pines, thereby debarking the trees. Soon the light bone of the antlers changes to a rich brown color as plant juice and debris are rubbed against them.

Although moose antlers are very large, especially those of the North American/East Siberian moose, relative to body mass they are only modest in size. Trophy bulls from Alaska average about 50 pounds (23 kg) in antler mass; Canadian bulls average about 44 pounds (20 kg), and small southern moose average about 35 pounds (16 kg). European moose, although as large as Canadian moose, average only about 22 pounds (10 kg) of antler mass in trophy

---

A bull testing a cow's urine. A bull allows the cow's urine to flow over its nose. It then curls back its upper lips, exposing the palate, and, while raising the head up, stands as if in a trance, with the head slowly moving to and fro. This behavior is called lip-curl, or by its German name *flehmen*. In the bull's palate is a small cleft leading to a special sensory organ, the Jacobson's organ. Scientists suspect that it allows the bull to judge a female's sexual receptiveness by her urine.

bulls. The largest moose antlers from Alaska weighed 79.2 pounds (36 kg). Antler growth is greatest in bulls six to ten years of age.

Whereas the size of the antlers is a function of age and the quality of the animal's nutrition, the symmetry of the antlers reflects the health of the animal. Antlers grow irregularly if a bull is wounded or if it has parasites or is diseased.

White-tailed deer and moose have about the same capacity to grow antlers. Those of caribou, however, are much larger relative to the body mass of the animal. In fact, caribou carry—relatively—the largest antlers of any deer species alive today.

Now that the antlers are fully developed, bull moose show more interest in one another and the first sparring matches develop. Slowly tipping their antlers from side to side, the bulls approach one another. The shiny antlers are important in signaling, and experiments in which observers held antlers and approached bulls confirm that bulls convey messages by the movements of their antlers. Antler waving is part of the dominance display of bulls and one of the rituals of courtship.

Dominance displays are indirect threats in which bull moose pull rank on one another. They are also tests of an opponent's resolve. Such displays always precede fights between large bulls. They also precede sparring matches, which are not fights but sporting engagements between befriended bulls. Sparring matches are not used to establish dominance. Such friendly rivalry only takes place between bulls with established rank, in which one is accepted as dominant and the other as subordinate. This understanding allows bulls of greatly differing body and antler sizes to spar with one another. Both partners are eager to engage in these tussles. No full-strength pushing results; instead the bulls, after carefully placing and replacing their antlers, twist with their necks. Then one of the bulls must step quickly aside to avoid severe neck twisting. Bulls often disengage only to engage again. In mule deer the sparring matches are extensive and serve to bond a master buck that controls a female clan with young bucks. The latter then form a protective shield about the master buck and his females, preventing other young bucks from interfering with the old buck. It is not clear, however, what advantages moose derive from these en-

gagements. One theory is that bulls learn the dimensions of their antlers while in velvet, and sparring helps to confirm this knowledge.

Sparring, though friendly and sporting, is not without danger. Some time ago when I visited Harvard's museum of comparative zoology, the locked antlers of two moose decorated the entrance. These were pointed out to me with the comment that

98

The velvet comes off last from the top of the antlers. The back surfaces of the antlers are stained darker than the front surfaces, as these are more likely to come in contact with vegetation during thrashing. This keeps the front of the antler showy, and is quite noticeable in the dim light of dusk and dawn when the bulls are most active. A bloody antler just cleared of velvet spells the end of "vacation" and the beginning of hard, serious, dangerous work. The bulls have prepared all year for this. They must breed in the next six weeks—or wait another year for a chance.

Sparring is a sporting engagement between friends. These bulls are "on sparring terms"—sparring is not fighting, even though it may superficially look like such. In sparring, bulls invite each other by lowering and presenting the antlers, then disengage and look away—this is a ritualized form of temporarily terminating sparring, and is understood as such by all concerned. Sparring bulls rarely push, but more often engage antlers carefully and twist necks. Sometimes a bull spars with one antler only. By comparison, dominance fights by matched bulls are violent. Bulls clash onto one another, which they do not do in sparring. Injury is common in fights, with active bulls receiving thirty to fifty antler punctures each season. It's thus little wonder that successful bulls are exhausted by the rut, as they must also heal these deep, pus-filled punctures.

A fine yearling bull scraping off dead and dying velvet from his antlers. Note the blood and the white bone, as well as the damaged bark on the spruce. The resin of the spruce will trap a few hairs, evidence that a moose, not an elk, did the damage.

they had died fighting. They almost certainly did not. The two sets of antlers were greatly mismatched. Those of the young bull were placed well within the larger set of the old bull. They locked antlers not in a fight for dominance, but in a friendly sparring match that came to an unexpected and tragic end. These were not the antlers of rivals, but of friends.

Fighting, in contrast to sparring, is a true test of dominance between bulls. It is very different from the careful neck twisting of a sparring match. A fight is initiated with dominance displays. The rivals approach at a tangent. The antlers are tipped slowly but conspicuously. The ears are laid back. The bulls view each other by twisting their eyes in their sockets while slightly averting their heads. The movements are slow, deliberate, and muscle-bound. The hooves barely clear the ground. When an early

ALL PHOTOS: The rutting pit or scrape sequence. The bull moose urinates copiously and repeatedly into a small scrape it paws with its front legs. Once the urine and soil are churned into a soft mud, the bull lowers its head to the scrape and, by striking downward with a front hoof, splashes the urine-soaked mud on its bell and lower antlers. The bell is a urine-scent-dispensing organ analogous to the neck mane of elk. The bull also lowers its body into the scrape, or rutting pit, and may rub his body in the mud. Cow moose get very excited over the urine scent of bulls. They not only lie down in the scrapes, but may try to displace bulls bedded in the scrape. Cows may fight over scrapes. The scent of a rutting pit is perfectly obvious to a human nose. After urinating, pawing, and dispensing scent, bulls may rise and horn small trees—advertising their presence much as males of other deer species do.

Bulls thrash to signal to rivals. They are also attracted to antler thrashing by other bulls. Only very confident bulls thrash loudly. This making of sound is somewhat comparable to the bugling of elk. Bull moose do not bugle or roar in the rut. Bulls do vocalize, but the call is soft, rhythmic, and not heard far off.

snowfall blankets the land, one can see from the tracks that large bull moose ponderously "drag" their hooves, just as white-tailed and mule deer bucks do. The thrashing of shrubs with antlers punctuates the approach. This too is a dominance display, as are the low "croaking" sounds made by approaching bulls. Antler engagement is not gradual and gentle as in sparring, but sudden and violent. There is little neck twisting; rather, the bulls engage in full-strength pushing and wrestling matches. If the ground is soft, as it is likely to be in moose habitat, the combatants may plow it up in their violent struggle. The method of disengagement resembles that of other deer that undertake frontal antler combat: the loser attempts to disengage by turning around, while the winner tries to gore him in that crucial moment.

The wounds sustained in fights between adult bulls may be severe, and combatants may show some thirty to fifty antler wounds at the end of the rut. Some of these wounds are long tears; others are punctures. Most are distributed over the face, neck, and rear of the moose. In addition to antler tears and punctures, cuts occur when moose collide with sharp, dry twigs and branches as they crash through

Rutting moose in Baxter State Park, Maine. Cows appear to select water for calling and attracting bulls with the sound of their urinating in the water. Calls also carry farther over open water than through dense forests.

BOTH PHOTOS: A prime, old woodland bull cautiously courts a cow, lip-curling on her urine. He ignores the inquisitive calf. He is experienced, confident, and thus well accepted by the cow.

dense shrubbery and windfalls. In ranch country, moose may be badly scarred by barbwire as they plow into fences. The thick skin of a rutting bull moose is, clearly, an asset. The antlers are also important in fending off injury. One large bull I autopsied shortly after the rut had broken off an antler and was extensively scarred on the side the antler was missing. At least one of the wounds was infected.

Finding a Mate

By the first week of September, roaming bull moose have found cows and are consorting with them. Sometimes two or more bulls attend one cow. Smaller bulls keep their distance from larger bulls, and yearling bulls may be chased off by the cows.

Large bulls move slowly, stopping frequently to display their dominance. The cows follow these big bulls. Unlike an elk or a red deer stag, a bull moose does not vocalize loudly to advertise its presence. It is the bull's olfactory signals that play a crucial part in attracting cows. A dominant bull moose roams over a fairly large area within which it sets scent markers. It does this by pawing the ground with its front legs. The bull then bends down and urinates into the scrape it has made. It repeats the process several times. Then it lowers its head into the scrape and smacks the urine-soaked earth with a front hoof so that it sprays in all directions. The mud sticks to the underside of the bull's head—that is, the bell of the moose—and to the lower parts of the neck and antlers. The bull thus transfers urine scent from the ground to the bell, which seems to act as a scent-dispensing organ.

The bell's function was long a mystery. It is a dangling flap of skin generously covered with fairly long hair. In the bull it comprises the "bag" and the "rope"; cows have "ropes" only. The rope may be very short or very long, and it appears to freeze off in cold winters. Consequently, one sees impressive ropes only where the winters are relatively mild, and only on young bulls. The bag grows directly underneath the lower jaw. It is inconspicuous on young bulls and prominent on old ones. There are no conspicuous glands on the bell. Although the bull moose does not wallow exuberantly in its urine-soaked scrape, as do bull elk or red deer stags, it does settle down into the wallow and rub its body in the scrape. Thus not only the bell, but also the body hair of the bull picks up the urine scent.

Cow moose are greatly stimulated by the urine scent of a rutting bull. They may fight rival females for the privilege of lowering themselves into a urine-soaked scrape. While he is urinating into the scrape, the bull greatly excites any cows in his presence, and these may run in circles around him, sometimes hitting his sides and belly with their heads. This suggests that the bull's scent advances estrous; it probably also bonds the cows to him. Cow moose follow big bulls as they move off from their scrapes. Unlike males in some other species of deer, the bull moose does not herd harems of cows, but consorts with one female at a time. After breeding is completed, the bull leaves this female to search for another mate. Occasionally several cow moose consort with one bull, and cows may compete aggressively with one another for a favorite bull.

Both the cow and the bull contribute to pair bonding until copulation. The cow moose has a distinctive mating call that attracts bulls from a considerable distance. Because moose may be hidden in shrubbery or widely spaced in wilderness regions, the mating call of the female helps the two sexes make contact. The cow also vocalizes softly when the bull is courting her, and the bull moose vocalizes softly when approaching the female during courtship. The same sound, uttered more loudly and harshly, is used by a displaying bull when it approaches rivals. This call is uttered at each alternate step. That is, the bull utters a loud grunt at a rival, then repeats it whenever his left (or right) front foot hits the ground during his approach.

The bull moose displays while in the presence of the cow. It makes itself large and conspicuous, keeping broadside to the cow, while moving the tips of its antlers from side to side. Occasionally, it utters a soft grunt. Cow moose are not only large, but also aggressive. Thus the dominance display of the bull is sensible in this context. It is clear that cows prefer

An older bull from Maine watches a cow in a pond. Once a pair forms, they follow one another until after mating.

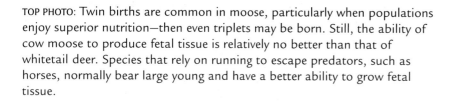

TOP PHOTO: Twin births are common in moose, particularly when populations enjoy superior nutrition—then even triplets may be born. Still, the ability of cow moose to produce fetal tissue is relatively no better than that of whitetail deer. Species that rely on running to escape predators, such as horses, normally bear large young and have a better ability to grow fetal tissue.

BOTTOM PHOTO: Moose of both sexes and all ages love to play—especially with water. They attack water, using the species-specific defensive threat, lashing out with both front and hind legs. They may run, splashing water into big sheets. Play is most common in individuals that are growing, and therefore adults play most often in early summer. Calves and yearlings play during all but the most strenuous parts of the year. Play is essential to good body growth.

Calves are generally born in the last week in May or the first week in June. They usually weigh 22 to 35 pounds (10–16 kg) at birth. Most adult cows have a calf or two at heel; however, very few of the newborns will survive the first two months of life, due to predation by grizzly bears, black bears, and wolves. This happens despite the well-earned reputation of cow moose for violence.

adult bulls to yearlings, but it is not clear whether they prefer large-antlered bulls to small-antlered bulls. When the bull switches to courting the cow, he approaches her with his head extended, softly grunting. Then he sniffs and licks the vulva. The female may urinate, and the bull then performs the lip-curl. After licking the urine, the bull raises its head high, pulls back the upper lip, and slowly waves its head from side to side. It is likely testing the urine for metabolic products that indicate the approach of estrous. It does this by passing the urine over its Jacobson's organ, which is located in the upper palate. This testing of the female's urine by means of a lip-curl is almost universal in male ungulates. The bull's soft vocalizations during the courtship approach are reminiscent of a calf in distress. Thus it appears that the bull manipulates the cow's maternal emotions to get close to her. Copulations are rarely witnessed in the wild.

The cow moose is polyestrous, meaning she may have several heat and ovulation periods, each about three weeks apart. Once she has bred successfully, the cycles stop. Most ovulations cluster in the last week of September, with about 10 percent occurring in the following heat period, in mid- to late October. The reason for these dates rests with the gestation period of moose, and the need to bear calves at a favorable time of the year. The larger a species of deer, the longer its gestation period. Moose, the largest New World deer, and elk, the largest species of Old World deer, have the longest gestation periods within their respective subfamilies. New World deer have a slightly shorter gestation period per unit of body weight than Old World deer, so that moose and elk ovulate at nearly the same time of year, even though the elk is smaller. The gestation period in moose averages 231 days, about 14 days less than in elk.

In Europe, the high point of the rut shifts from

112

mid-September in the south to mid-October in the north, and appears linked to the latitudinal differences in plant growth—earlier in the south, later in the north. Births must be timed to catch the eruption of plants, so that cows have enough feed available to produce a maximum amount of milk. The timing of the rut can also be influenced by the composition of the moose population: where the sex ratio of adult cows and bulls is near parity, the rut is advanced and condensed so that all calves are born close together and early in the year. This allows calves the maximum time to grow to survivable size. Where sex ratios are badly distorted and there are few bulls, the rut is extended because not all cows are bred on their first ovulation. Consequently, some calves may be born late in the year.

After the Rut

The rutting season of moose lasts about a month, although most breeding occurs within a three-week period. After the rut, bulls rest to recover their strength and to heal infected wounds. They have virtually no body fat left. Soon they form fraternal groups. Where moose densities are high, these groups are segregated by age: old bulls go with old bulls, young ones with young ones. The time is late October to early November. Snow now covers the ground and the leaves are long shed. Bull groups in open burns or in the willow flats of subalpine areas are an impressive sight. The largest fraternal group I saw numbered nineteen. All were small antlered—that is, fairly young bulls. These clubs fraternize after the animosity of the rut is over. The bulls still carry antlers, which allow them to spar every so often.

These fraternal groups assemble and reassemble. They last well into December and even early January. In mid-December the oldest bulls begin to shed their antlers. Afterwards, the exposed site where the antler was remains red for a day or two until the wound heals. Antler growth is then dormant until late March, when the antler buds form. With the shedding of the antlers, the fraternal groups begin to dissolve. Bulls that have lost their antlers become targets of dominance challenges by younger bulls. Some old bulls without antlers rush and chase off younger challengers. Others display back, then rear up on their hind legs and lash out with their front legs. In one case I observed, an old bull knocked an antler off a young bull. Antlers are part of a bull's personality. Without them it becomes a stranger to other bulls. Its rank can no longer be discerned. To escape repeated challenges, antlerless bulls disperse, moving off alone to some distant wintering ground.

Bulls lose their antlers at the end of the season of loose snow and low snow levels. From January onward snow levels rise and the snow becomes harder. It is thus advantageous for bulls to disperse before they are marooned in deep snow. As the snow deepens and increasingly restricts the movement of moose, some moose may reverse their solitary existence and yard up in deep snow with other moose. They use communal paths plowed in deep snow, though each moose feeds apart from others. Fairly large groups of moose may yard together. Others spend the winter in isolation along some shrub-lined creek at high elevation. Bulls in particular prefer high elevations.

Even with their antlers long dropped, North American bull moose are recognizable by their black noses and the large bags under their chins. Cows sport reddish brown noses and have no bell bags. Cows also have large whitish, triangular vulval patches under their tails. By observing these three characteristics, the sex of North American moose can be identified quite reliably. European moose, however, are not dimorphic for nose color. The noses of both sexes are quite dark. When American moose are shedding their coats, their sex cannot be determined by nose color either; however, at that time all bulls have started to grow antlers, and distinguishing cows from bulls is no great problem.

As the snow level increases toward late winter, the snow hardens and snow crusts form, impeding the movement of moose. Moose now obtain less food, though they feed less and less selectively. They must rely on body stores to survive. At this time of year moose are relatively weak. Captive moose feeding on their own in the taiga are not able to work as beasts of burden. Moose remain weak until well into summer. Those at high elevations may search out thermoclines—layers of warm air that form along mountain fronts. They also expose themselves to the winter sun, for they save half a calorie of fat for

BOTH PHOTOS: A mere fifteen months old, this bull moose is already sexually mature, as indicated by his shedding of antler velvet. He has the black-nosed bull's face. However, he is still chased off by cows he tries to court—as well as by older bulls.

every calorie of sunshine that is absorbed by their dark coats. And every calorie counts in this time of shortage.

Such animals, depleted and struggling to survive, cannot readily take the extra strains of disturbance caused by recreational skiing or snowmobiling. Moose are designed to live a very quiet life in winter, so they can survive on little food and limited supplies of body fat. Plowing in panic through snow to avoid people on skis or snowmobiles saps energy and life from moose who are struggling to stay alive.

The Next Generation

In winter, pregnant cow moose deplete reserves of fat built up during the summer months. If the summer feeding has gone well, the cows may well be carrying more than one calf. This is because under excellent feeding conditions, single calves are likely to grow very large inside their mothers. Such calves may cause problems at birth, particularly in young females. Large calves may get stuck in the birth canal.

If they are born, they may be damaged during the birth process and die, or they may be abandoned due to the pain they have caused their mothers. A cow moose that implants two embryos when food is abundant, on the other hand, will likely bear two calves of survivable size, suffer few if any birth complications, and contribute two calves to the population. Thus, in moose populations that have colonized rich habitats, cow moose are favored that give birth to twins. Conversely, when conditions are poor, the cow that implants only one embryo is more likely to bear a calf of survivable size. Such a calf need not share its mother's meager supply of milk with another calf and has a fair chance of growing to survivable size by fall. Clearly, cow moose need to be sensitive to forage conditions, implanting single embryos when conditions are poor, and implanting two eggs— or even three—when conditions are good. Natural selection will therefore favor adaptable cow moose.

In spring, the cow moose selects a secluded birth site where she will hide while her calf is very small. She even suckles her calf while lying down, a behavioral trait she shares only with reindeer, a close relative. Water sources are abundant where moose live, whether succulent forage, snow, or free-standing water. Unlike most dwellers of dry steppe, such as horses and camels, moose need not go to distant water holes to load up on the day's water. Consequently, a cow moose need not store water for her suckling young, as female horses or camels must. Moose thus produce fairly concentrated milk with milk solids amounting to 20 to 24 percent of volume. Horses and camels produce much more dilute milk. In horses' milk, solids are only 8 to 12 percent of volume.

The milk of the cow moose is richer in protein and fats than that of domestic cattle. Cow moose produce 220 to 440 pounds (100–200 kg) of milk in the four months after birth, which seems a modest amount. Nevertheless, calves grow from 24 to 35 pounds (11–16 kg) at birth to 260 to 330 pounds (120–150 kg) or more in four to five months. They may gain as much as 4.4 pounds (2 kg) a day. Size has priority over mass, as can be deduced from the fact that calves still have rather soft bones in the fall. The quicker the moose calf reaches adult proportions, the sooner it can clear tall obstacles and run swiftly over long distances.

Only an abundant supply of high-quality food in summer can insure that cow moose produce adequate amounts of the rich milk so essential for their calves' rapid growth. It appears that cows may defend pockets of rich food against other moose in the summer—such as a pocket of dense aquatic vegetation where a creek runs into a lake—and the intolerance cow moose with small calves display toward other moose may well be resource related.

Not all the cows' intolerance is related to resources, however. While they are growing to survivable size, calves need to be closely protected against predators by their mothers. In most deer species, the fawns have spotted coats to camouflage them when hiding from danger. Other than when they are first born, however, calf moose do not hide, but rather depend on their mothers for protection, making a spotted coat unnecessary. Cow moose are doting, ferocious mothers, and moose calves are extremely good at extracting every bit of care and attention from them. The devoted mother moose not only

An adult bull moose in rut in Grand Teton National Park, Wyoming, in late October. This bull was repeatedly approached by cows and shows little "rutting wear," such as wounds or antler marks in his coat. He is in exceptionally good condition.

attacks any bears and wolves that might come by, but also all other moose. In the first week or so of the calf's life, the mother moose chases away other moose. She does so not only to safeguard her food supply, but also because small calves are not selective in whom they follow; any large moving object will do. Therefore, the cow cannot tolerate other large animals in the vicinity until the calf is firmly bonded to her. If a cow moose is separated from her calf for ten days or more, she will reject her calf if they are reunited. To keep its mother close, the calf may call in a plaintive voice when the cow wanders too far off, if the calf faces an obstacle, or if the mother enters a river or lake to swim. The calves initially are reluctant to enter streams and lakes, and may complain bitterly even when swimming after mother.

Observations of young captive moose suggest that moose are programmed for learning and that their early experiences have a profound influence on them. Young moose kept in groups imitate one another and can be taught by a keeper to strip bark from trees. Calves raised with dogs become vulnerable to wolf predation. Moose bonded to humans readily accept foods that wild moose will not touch, including various livestock feeds, as well as orchard, garden, and houseplants.

Family Ties

The enduring bond between a hand-raised moose and its keeper is almost certainly related to the way cow moose share space and resources with their sons and daughters in the wild. Other New World deer form maternal clans that defend feeding areas. In white-tailed deer, mothers may allow adult daughters preferential use of their territories. I suspect something similar happens with moose. Young moose raised together form closed groups that repel strangers. That is suggestive. Some cow moose raised together form such close bonds that they allow other members of the group to lick their new-

After the rut is over, bulls once again join up with one another. Sparring is then a common sport. It lasts long into winter, until the bulls begin to drop their antlers in December, and—in most areas—disperse to a solitary life thereafter.

born calves. This is remarkable, since cows normally form individual birth territories. Perhaps cow moose also give their daughters, and perhaps even their sons, preferential access to resources on the maternal home range. This would be particularly important in low-density populations with low rates of reproduction.

Under good conditions, cow moose bear calves every year. Under poor conditions, however, a cow that raises a calf to a survivable size by early fall may be too thin to ovulate, or too thin for the egg to implant. She will not bear a calf the following spring. In this case, it pays to continue parenting the yearling so as to maximize its chances of survival. In short, under good conditions cows and yearlings separate; under marginal conditions yearlings follow their dams in their second summer of life. The often violent separation of a pregnant cow and her yearling favors the dispersal of moose and the colonization of vacant habitat; the extension of care to yearlings favors the transmission of home-range knowledge from mother to offspring. When food is scarce over a wide area, the yearling learns more from its mother about where to feed during different seasons, and is thus more likely to survive and thrive.

In normal years, the separation of yearlings from pregnant moose proceeds fairly rapidly in late spring. The process is a sudden one, as the cow needs to protect her child as long as possible against predators. Consequently, she chases it off as late as possible, usually about two weeks before she gives birth. When the cow first shows signs of hostility toward her yearling, the child does not take her threats seriously. When she becomes more forceful and rushes the yearling, it evades the charge in playful gambols and returns right away to mother. Again it is chased off. After a few such dismissals, the yearling appears perplexed. It stays a little distance behind the cow, watches her, but follows. The cow moves off, and as the yearling follows, she turns on it again. She may come to blows. The distance between mother and child increases noticeably. The yearling peeks after its mother as shrubs obscure her. It follows her, but much more timidly. When surprised by the cow, it runs off, stops, and retraces its steps. And so it goes for a day or two, until the yearling finally wanders off alone. It feeds little and searches out the com-

pany of other yearlings. I have seen up to eight yearlings form a temporary group.

Abandoned yearlings often attempt to follow other moose. Adult cows chase them off at once; bulls are more tolerant. I once observed a big bull and a calf commence a sparring match. The little yearling was so eager. The big bull was game, but it also tried to protect its soft, tender antlers by pushing back with its cheek and the side of its head

After the excitement and competition of the rutting season, bull moose in large populations once again join into bachelor clubs and stay together until they shed their antlers. As long as they have antlers, the bulls spar good naturedly. Once the antlers drop and sparring is impossible, moose disperse. This happens just before deep, hard snow packs make gregarious life dangerous. Over much of their range, moose in late winter are stranded in deep snow, and where a single moose can live, a group would quickly deplete the limited browse.

This young bull has dropped one antler, and the antler pedicle is well into healing and being overgrown by a protective skin. It will form the next antler bud. The bull is cutting off a willow twig with its premolars.

against the yearling's face and front. Suddenly the bull jerked back as if in pain. In a flash it raised a front leg and struck the yearling, which bolted back in pain and surprise. Right there they parted company. Clearly, the tolerance of the bull had its limits.

The yearling moose learn quickly after being rejected by their mothers, and their attempts to stay close to adult moose become less and less frequent as the days pass. In a few short months they must find high-quality feeding sites, and they must remember to return to wintering grounds before being immobilized in deep snow. Many yearlings stumble on underused burn habitat, and prosper. Some, however, are unable to grow large and fatten adequately before winter. These moose will fall prey to wolves. A small drop in body size can cause the balance in the moose–wolf equation to tip greatly in favor of the wolf.

The newly independent yearlings feed and rest alone, play in the meadows in the morning and evening, and move about a lot. When hand-raised moose near adulthood they often leave home for days or weeks on end. These moose then show up at other farms and forestry stations. About half of the roaming yearlings on Russian moose farms fail to return. This dispersal behavior matches that of young moose in the wild.

Yearling moose are not terribly shy. They stop to examine matters of interest and may show little fear of humans. It is such yearlings that show up in cities in late spring. Once they learn to associate people with food, they search people out, raid gardens, or become aggressive with passersby. Moose in cities may disrupt traffic, break down fences, and cause a commotion until they are caught and removed to safety. A few learn how to make a living in the city, as did two young bulls that settled on an island in the Bow River in Calgary, Alberta, Canada, a few years ago. They were a welcome sight to the public, until fall, when they polished their little antlers and, under the command of the rutting season, began to roam the city. One collapsed and died as it tried to evade captors; the other received a fatal overdose of immobilizing drugs as officials tried to corner it.

The rapid, even violent, disassociation of yearling moose from their mothers is truly a remarkable

The shed antlers of moose first bleach due to sun and rain. Slowly they disintegrate, hastened on their way by rodents, rabbits, and porcupines gnawing at the bone.

form of separation. In American mountain sheep, which live on tiny patches of discontinuous mountain grasslands, the separation of mothers and yearlings is a gradual process that lasts about two months. The yearling sheep are never chased off or disturbed. They remain on their mothers' home ranges. To strike out into the unknown would be futile for yearling sheep. They would risk getting lost in the forest, for the acceptable areas of habitat are small indeed. Moreover, all acceptable habitat already is known to the population, so the best way to acquire such knowledge is to follow an adult. Mountain sheep make every effort to keep the yearlings on the female home range when the mothers move off to bear lambs.

In moose, however, rapid disassociation appears to contribute to the yearlings' distraught wandering. This appears to be an adaptive feature. In a growing moose population it insures the dispersal of yearlings, and thus the colonization of new, unexploited habitat. When life is good for moose, the violence of the cow moose toward her yearling helps to foster dispersal and to colonize new habitat. When life is

bad, cow moose act more like female mountain sheep and retain their yearlings through the spring and summer.

Moose are deer, and like most deer species, they benefit from ecological turmoil. That is why deer prospered in the ecological havoc caused by the ice ages, and that is why they have succeeded so well in the last two million years when other large herbivores have failed. Moose live by destructive and life-rejuvenating forces such as the flooding, silting, and ice scouring of rivers; by the havoc of forest fires; by the tree-shredding ravages of avalanches and forest-flattening ice storms—natural calamities all. The biology of moose has evolved to benefit from natural catastrophes that reverse the cycle of ecological maturation and return the land to an earlier, younger, and more productive phase. In different regions and over time, these catastrophes generate different compositions of shrubs and young trees. The adaptable moose, with its catholic food habits, is well suited to exploit these various plant communities. Calamities are a guarantee that moose will prosper—provided people let them.

 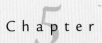

Moose and People

How moose have survived and prospered in northern Eurasia and North America is a complex story. Their survival is not merely a consequence of their high reproductive rates, their inclination to disperse and probe for new living space, their ability to learn, and their sensitivity as adults to human dangers. These biological attributes have undoubtedly helped moose to survive, but biological resistance will not be enough to ensure their continued survival in the modern era. Moose thrive on fires, floods, avalanches, and disasters to their foes, but ultimately their survival will depend on their interactions with human beings.

The Hunter and the Hunted

When Columbus landed in America in 1492, Europe and Asia were not continents of wilderness—and neither was North America. The land served the native human inhabitants. Wildlife was managed if it was valuable to local tribes, and within their power to control. Otherwise it was left to fend for itself, hunted opportunistically, and exterminated locally or continentally. Although the size of North America's pre-Columbian native population remains a subject of debate, recent studies suggest that a large human population extracted sustenance from the land to the limits of available technology.

A wary bull watches the world from the shelter of a lodgepole pine forest in Yellowstone National Park.

That humans entered North America at all is something of a miracle. Whereas *Homo sapiens* had colonized Africa, Asia, Europe, Australia, and South America by about forty thousand years ago, humans did not cross the Bering land bridge and establish themselves in North America until about eleven thousand years ago. In North America, a multitude of specialized herbivore species left little plant food for humans to exploit, while several species of large, ever-hungry predators made existence impossible for hunters armed only with stone-tipped spears. Only after the extinction of the biggest predator—the bull-dog bear, which stood as tall as a moose at the shoulders—did humans colonize North America. Why the bulldog bear died out about twelve thousand years ago is unknown; however, by that date humans had domesticated the dog and this makes it possible—in theory—that humans used dogs to distract the big bear and then kill it, much as Inuit hunters killed polar bears with dogs and lances. There is no evidence, but human hunters may have contributed to the extinction of this formidable predator.

Once humans settled North America, it took only five hundred years for them to eliminate the Colombian mammoth. After the Colombian mammoth, human hunters turned next to the indigenous long-horned bison. It held out for about eight hundred years, then was replaced by a smaller Siberian bison. As the influence of human hunters persisted and the climate warmed, the native megafauna of the Pleistocene era collapsed. Siberian species previously barred from the lower parts of North America by superior competitors and predators now colonized the continent. Those that arrived before the Bering land bridge finally flooded eight thousand years ago included the elk, the grizzly bear, the gray wolf, and the moose.

The archeological record indicates that human existence in North America before the arrival of Columbus was marked by bitter hunger. Humans can live well on the fat meat of large northern mammals, but the lean meat of small mammals must be supplemented by plant food or the meat of fat fish. Early hunter-gatherers concentrated on large herbivores as prey, and this resulted in the local extinctions of bison, elk, and moose. Hunting-gathering was followed by agriculture, which began about seven thou-sand years ago in the highlands of Central America, spreading northward over southern and eastern North America. Large animals and agriculture are not compatible. Where intensive agriculture spread over the land, large herbivores such as bison, elk, and moose—and the large carnivores that fed on them—vanished.

After Columbus landed, Old World diseases and genocide rapidly decimated native populations. Unchecked by human predation, wildlife multiplied and spread, and so did forests that had been restricted by fires set by the native populations. Early European explorers witnessed this rebound of nature and formed an image of pre-Columbian America as a wilderness with bountiful wildlife and few people. They were fooled into believing that America was a natural land untouched by human hand. Yet this wilderness was actually a biotic response to three absences: the absence of a native megafauna, the absence of human predation, and the absence of agricultural alterations to the landscape. This rebound of nature lasted until about 1850, by which time white settlers had ended it all.

How many moose there are in the world depends on human interactions with moose. This has been the case in the past, and will continue to be the case in the future. A look at the cycles of moose populations in North America since the arrival of the first human settlers illustrates the point. Before the arrival of Columbus, moose were virtually absent wherever native populations were high. Their populations then rebounded when diseases and conflicts decimated natives. In the North, moose numbers declined in response to the needs of the fur trade. As native populations and the fur trade dwindled, moose populations recovered. The huge forest fires that accompanied the development of gold mines and railway lines aided this recovery; it was hindered by hunters who supplied meat to the gold mines and to the settlements that the railway served.

In the nineteenth century, American military policy aimed to subdue native people by eliminating wildlife. In this the military strategists were largely successful, and by 1900, wildlife and native populations had declined to their nadir. Then, in the period leading up to World War I, new ideas, such as national parks, commissions on conservation, inter-

Moose tame easily. In the past, they made fine beasts of burden, mounts, and milkers for people in Eurasia. Raised by caring humans, moose act more like loyal dogs than like wild deer. However, they are difficult to keep in captivity because they are sensitive to livestock diseases and survive poorly on livestock feeds. These moose in Wyoming have obviously come to the right place for food.

A prime bull, early in the rut carelessly crosses a road. Bulls are less wary during the rut than before or after.

national wildlife treaties, and the elimination of wildlife as a trade commodity, led to modern North American wildlife conservation. This resulted in a deliberate restoration of wildlife continentwide in the twentieth century. Moose were major beneficiaries of this process. Today they are abundant in North America and spread over a greater range than ever before, not because of expansive wilderness or the grace of God, but because of government policies of wildlife management over the past eighty years.

Moose have also benefited from the ecological havoc caused by modern society. Three factors in particular have favored moose: the increased frequency of forest fires, large-scale logging, and the abandonment of unproductive farmland at the forest fringes that subsequently reverted to early-growth forests. Thanks to laws controlling hunting, reintroduction programs, natural disasters, and changes in land use, moose populations in North America today are relatively healthy.

Experiments in Domestication

In North America, the moose has generally been seen as an animal to be hunted. In Eurasia, people have always hunted moose, but they have also attempted to exploit them in other ways. In the Middle Stone Age (about six thousand to ten thousand years ago) conditions in Europe were desperate for humans. People had to learn to fish and to find food in the dense forests that sprang up where hordes of reindeer, horses, and long-horned bison had once roamed the open, windswept steppe. Cannibalism and murder were widespread, people were poorly grown and diseased, tools were diverse but of poor workmanship, and art was all but forgotten. The rise of agriculture with the New Stone Age (about four thousand to seven thousand years ago) brought relief—as it had done in North America.

Reindeer, a close relative of the moose, were probably first domesticated some nine thousand years ago. As highly social mammals whose males settled their rivalries and remained together—as opposed to establishing territories and thereby distancing and isolating themselves from one another—reindeer were good candidates for domestication. Large herds of domestic reindeer sustained northern populations in Europe and Asia, providing milk,

ABOVE: A hussar mounted on a moose, the hoped-for secret weapon of the Swedish cavalry in the 1700s. Horses that have never seen or smelled a moose go berserk at the sight of them. This would allow the Swedish cavalry to rout their enemies. The experiment was not a success, however, as moose, excellent mounts though they are, are difficult to keep in captivity.

FACING PAGE: The moose nose is a great delicacy among native hunters. After the hair is singed and scraped off, the nose is roasted slowly at the edge of a hot bed of coals. Moose nose can also be transformed into a superlative head cheese. After it is boiled, and the hair is scraped and rinsed off, it is placed into a pot with fresh water and selected vegetables. The gelatin boiled from the nose is exceptionally stiff, and the result is well worth the mess.

ABOVE: Bulls greatly vary not only in the structure of antlers, but also of the bell.

RIGHT: Moose and white-tailed deer are close relatives. The white-tailed deer is the older species, one adapted to southern latitudes where many diseases and parasites are found. Moose coexist with white-tailed deer only where a good ecological segregation is possible, because white-tailed deer pass on three devastating parasites to moose: the meningeal worm, the winter tick, and the giant liver fluke. The meningeal worm settles on the brain of whitetails, where it produces larvae without too much distress to the host. In moose, however, the adult worms are somehow unable to settle on the brain. They traverse the brain tissue and destroy the brain in the process. Afflicted moose die a slow death. Winter ticks multiply on moose boundlessly and in severe cases may denude a moose of most winter fur. Such naked moose are called ghost moose. Moose adapted to cold East Siberian conditions are poorly protected against the illnesses of southern relatives or of livestock. They rarely live long in zoos.

Moose are attracted to groomed trails with low, hard snow. They are creatures enslaved to the law of least effort. In the case of wintering moose, the reduction in effort plowing through deep snow is significant. However, and this may be more important, secure footing is vital for a moose defending itself. When danger threatens, moose choose hard, flat ground, because here they can flail and kick with front and hind legs in all directions. This is how moose defend themselves against wolves. Moose on groomed trails are reluctant to leave even when approached by well-meaning people.

meat, and hides, and also serving as beasts of burden. Moose in Europe have served similar purposes, except that moose cannot be herded, they do not roam, and the results of domesticating them over the centuries have been mixed.

In northern Europe and Asia moose were used, among other things, to carry riders and loads across inhospitable terrain. As a mount the moose has no equal in crossing bogs and windfalls, slipping through thickets, climbing over rocks, and swimming swiftly across broad, dangerous rivers. In the dense coniferous forests and bogs that cover much of northern Europe and Asia, a rider on horseback cannot outrun a rider on a moose—as Russian general Jermak Timofeitsch found out when he began the conquest of Siberia on behalf of Czar Ivan the Terrible in the sixteenth century. To gain the upper

hand over the Siberian moose riders, General Timofeitsch banned moose husbandry, killed off domesticated moose, and systematically hunted down moose riders to flay, impale, or mutilate them publicly as examples to others. It is likely that moose husbandry in the northern forests was just frequent enough to be a nuisance, since as we now know moose—for all their advantages as beasts of burden—are difficult to keep in captivity. Had trained moose been common and easy wards, the tough, adventuresome Cossacks would surely have changed mounts and pursued the moose riders on equal terms.

European moose were also used to pull sleighs great distances across frozen wastes. One drawback to using moose in this way is that horses unacquainted with moose shy wildly and become uncontrollable when confronted by these strange-looking

Tame cow moose can be trained for milking. This requires the removal of the newborn calf, so that the cow does not bond to the calf. Then the cow moose extends its affection to its keeper and will reject calves in later years. In such cows the lactation period can be extended gradually, increasing annual milk production from 220 to 440 pounds (100–200 kg) to more than 880 pounds (400 kg). Such cow moose are very loyal to their keepers and show up punctually every day for supplemental feeding and milking.

creatures. Thus, in the seventeenth century, the city council of the Estonian town of Dorpat (Tartu) forbade domesticated moose on its streets. One can only imagine what havoc horses out of control, hitched to a coach or wagon, could wreak in the town's narrow streets after suddenly coming face to face with a moose innocently pulling a sleigh into town.

King Karl XI of Sweden considered mounting a cavalry regiment on moose, probably to take advantage of the terror they would strike into the hearts of enemy horses. No canon and musket fire, no lances and sabers would be needed to disperse the enemy's cavalry charge. The mere appearance of moose on the battleground would put the enemy's cavalry into heedless flight. Alas, the king's grand plan came to naught, and experiments in domesticating moose in this century make it evident why. Moose could never

prosper as cavalry mounts because of their catastrophic susceptibility to livestock diseases, and because of the great difficulties in feeding moose properly.

After the seventeenth century, moose husbandry became a forgotten art for nearly four hundred years. An attempt in modern Sweden to train moose to the sleigh met with failure, casting grave doubt on the historical accounts that moose could be useful beasts of burden. Beginning in the 1930s, however, Russian scientists tackled the issue of moose husbandry systematically—and were successful. They discovered that moose could be trained to give milk, carry loads or riders, pull sleds and logs, go to pasture, and return willingly to stables.

A fully grown moose can carry about 275 pounds (125 kg) and work with a sleigh laden with 600 to

800 pounds (300–400 kg); it can pull a heavier sleigh, but not all day. Its walking speed is 1.8 to 2.5 miles per hour (3–4 km/h), and the comfortable working range in a four- to six-hour working day is about 12.5 miles (20 km). Greater performances are possible. Moose can carry packs through the roughest of terrain without doing the slightest damage to the pack. They crawl under windfalls, slither across swamps, jump obstacles, negotiate thickets, and swim torrents. Yet at the end of the day, the packs remain securely in place. Hand-reared moose have utter faith in their trainers. They will, for instance, calmly walk up to an aircraft whose engines are howling. Cow moose trained for milking shower their keepers with affection—a "problem" that, in one form or another, has been reported by all keepers of moose. The most useful working moose, not surprisingly, are castrated bulls, which grow large and strong and are easy to handle. Those who have kept tame moose report that the experience is more like keeping a friendly, loyal dog (one six feet [2 m] high at the shoulder) than like hosting a member of the deer family.

Although moose are useful and have some endearing characteristics, one reason they were never domesticated is that they are notoriously difficult to feed and keep healthy in captivity. Attempts by Russian scientists to subsidize the natural forage of moose with oats, barley, and wheatgerm failed as the moose became ill. What work the moose did perform was sustained by natural forages. Today, we know that the natural diet of moose can be supplemented with oat mash, beets, and potatoes; however, disease remains a problem. Moose are not only susceptible to livestock diseases, but also to the diseases of other deer species. American moose have an especially dismal record in captivity.

In North America moose are affected by meningeal worm, a nematode that dwells happily on the brain of white-tailed deer, but destroys the brain of infected moose. Deer ticks transferred to moose multiply rapidly and can cause major—and fatal—hair loss to moose in winter. These partially naked moose are known as ghost moose in Canada. In addition, the giant liver fluke of white-tailed deer may become a burden to moose. Where wild white-tailed deer are afflicted with these parasites, moose populations cannot survive. Caribou are similarly affected, while elk survive but do poorly.

Aside from the problems of nutrition and disease, the other argument against the domestication of moose is that they cannot be worked year round. In late winter, spring, and early summer, they are thin and weak and cannot be used as beasts of burden on natural forages alone. Except in limited circumstances, there seem to be more disadvantages than advantages to domesticating moose. There are, however, a number of documented cases of moose being kept as "pets."

The Nature of Moose

Moose usually come into human hands as newborn calves. If the calf is less than seven days old, it will immediately accept a keeper as its mother. A calf more than a week old will flee from approaching humans and requires much more work to tame; imprinting after fourteen days of age is impossible. Old moose may not tame at all, are severely stressed by capture, and may die of heart failure.

People who have raised moose in Scandinavia, Russia, Germany, or my home country of Canada have left detailed accounts of their experiences. Bottle-fed moose that had the run of a farm or a forestry station, and thus mingled human care and affection with access to natural forage, kept well in captivity. They became very tame, acting somewhat like giant dogs. Although tame bulls in rut are not easy to handle, they do not go out of their way to murder their keepers, as the bottle-fed males of some other species of deer do. Apparently, hand-raised bull moose do not see humans as rivals that must be attacked. Indeed, two that I observed actively courted people, treating them as potential mates. One even ejaculated. It got no further, though, as the keeper quickly fled its loving advances.

A bull feeds on deep-growing aquatic plants. Moose may even dive for food, which no other deer is known to do. By exploiting aquatic food, moose have become good survivors—a highly successful, abundant, productive, and widely distributed deer.

A moose calf left unattended for too long will cry out for its mother. Its cries are so penetrating that the natural response is to drop everything and run—not walk—to comfort the little moose. After all, in the wild, the calf's sole hope of survival is to stay close to its huge, well-armed, and devoted mother. Calves separated from their mothers soon fall prey to bears or wolves. Consequently, the calf seeks to be close to its mother at all times, whether that mother is its natural mother or a human substitute. It fears loneliness, and its cry for company is designed by nature to distress. This distress call works as effectively on the calf's human foster parent as it does on its natural mother.

Since orphan moose can hardly be kept isolated in some stable and thrive, they usually wind up inside the house, where they happily share space with cats, dogs, children, and other occupants. The fireplace is a universally favorite place for rest. A baby moose knows a good thing when it finds it, and the moose quickly becomes a fixture within the house, a member of the family. It worms its way into everyone's affections just like a puppy—albeit a rather large one.

A moose calf is programmed to learn and is consumed by curiosity. Its exploration of the household is total and involves smelling, tasting, and trying to move everything. This passion for learning cannot be quenched. The calf wants to know everything, and it wants to know it now. Nothing is safe from its curious nose. Flowers smell interesting and taste great. Flower vases can be pushed to the floor. Pea soup, pot roasts, gravy, and potatoes are tasted and dethroned from the kitchen table; dish towels and aprons are tasted and found unpalatable—eventually.

On the positive side, the long-legged and clumsy-looking youngster is a surprisingly good and quick learner. It can even be housebroken. One baby bull, after discovering that it was barred from the house when it had muddy feet, quickly learned to raise its muddy hooves and call for help until they were wiped clean. Baby moose explore house and cellar, garden and orchard, playpen and garage with determination and zeal. They become habituated to artificial structures and, adult moose readily enter barns to seek refuge from flies or to give birth to their calves. Moose have a good sense of time and, if they are free to roam, will return at regular hours for feeding and milking.

Anything of interest to the foster parent is at once of interest to the moose. Yet, moose also develop cravings all of their own. They may, for instance, become addicted to gasoline and exhaust fumes. One tame moose threw herself behind cars with running engines and inhaled deeply until she passed out. One of my friends who raised a moose had to brace for competition when it was time to tank up his jeep. The moment the hand pump clanked onto the 45-gallon (180-l) gasoline drum, his ward came tearing out of the bushes, or wherever she might be, and shot between him and the pump. Her big nose descended to the opening that contained the intoxicating fumes and she inhaled deeply—shoving my friend aside. It was a constant challenge to outwit the moose until the jeep could be fueled. Tame moose may also scrape and wallow over other strong-smelling substances, such as lavender oil or freshly felled conifers. To date, there is no explanation for this.

A young moose forms close bonds with the person that feeds and cares for it, and it retains these bonds into adult life. A moose is also loyal to the voice of the person who raised it. People who experimented with domesticating moose found that horns had to be used to control groups of moose, because each moose would respond only to voice commands given by its personal keeper. Hand-raised moose recognize their keepers even after extended periods of separation. One moose, after being separated from its foster parent for two and a half years, approached unhesitatingly the instant she recognized him. This bonding becomes extreme in females that are always milked by the same person. Such cows may abandon, or even kill, their newborn calves and extend their affections to their keepers.

Orphaned moose grow rapidly under the care and attention they extract from their keepers. As they balloon in size—and strength—they become increasingly more noticeable around the house. With a moose in a room, space shrinks quickly. When a calf is the size of a retriever, there is no space problem; however, moose do not remain the size of retrievers

A bull moose thrashes a willow bush.

for long. Young moose have astonishing growth rates. In a mere six months, a moose calf may weigh 330 pounds (150 kg) or more. Inevitably, the day comes when the calf must be banished from the house, as it fills the room and can barely squeeze through the door.

When the moose is denied entry, and evening comes without the cozy fireplace, without the companionship of other warm bodies, without the murmur of familiar voices and the reassuring scent of family and mother, a heartrending wailing starts. When a moose cries in sorrow, all who hear it suffer. Its cries are loud, they are plaintive, and they last a long, long time. Separation from mother—even a temporary separation—is sheer terror to the moose, and the banished moose uses every opportunity to make its feelings clear. During the night, it is likely to settle down right at the door, as close as it can come to the once-friendly room. There it sits—abandoned, innocent, and uncomprehending—and gives vent to its deep sorrow. All night long. The family of a friend who raised a moose suffered for three days and nights before their adopted child accepted the inevitable and settled into a new routine—blocking the rear door of the house every night. That was the closest it could get to "mother."

Another agony befell the adopted moose when my friend's children had to be delivered to a country school. Its foster parent drove off with the children, leaving it behind, alone. Bawling, the moose ran alongside until the car sped off. Still it ran on, until it was forced to stop from exhaustion. It returned to the spot where it had lost "mother" and waited until the car returned. A slightly less dramatic version of this event repeated itself every school day. The time of separation was followed by one of celebration when "mother" returned. And a moose does not stint when showing its happiness. One Prussian forester who had raised a female moose was in a boat on a canal one day when he was discovered by his "child." She had gone on a hike and had not seen "mother" for several days. She dove into the water, tried to climb into the boat, rolled the boat over, and smothered the man—who was by now swimming for his life—with affection.

This strange animal with the ungainly face can be quick witted, affectionate, and loyal to a fault. The forester's cow moose became a faithful hunting companion. Nose to the ground, she could unerringly track down her foster parent with a speed and precision that astounded experienced trainers of hunting dogs. She was not in the least gun-shy, ran to the sound of gunfire to find "mother," and complained of being left behind when the forester left with gun in hand. When the forester and his family moved to a different district, she searched until she found him. When she was rebuffed, as her presence failed to mesh with gardens and orchards, she quickly learned that she was not welcome. After her banishment, tracks marked her occasional nightly visits to both the forester's new home and his old one. And that, too, is in the nature of moose. No matter how close the bond between the baby moose and its mother, just before its first birthday comes the day of inevitable parting, when the young moose is driven off by its mother and must begin the lonely life of an adult. Mother is about to give birth again, and the yearling must not interfere with the raising of the new baby. Dear as her foster parents were, the adopted moose knew when she was dismissed for good, and she accepted her situation—except for an occasional nightly visit to stand beside the familiar house and her beloved people before moving back into the darkness of the forest.

Planning for the Future

Generally, moose thrive where humans derive utility from them. Where moose are useful, people are interested in them and informed about them. When people take an informed interest in moose, they work hard to protect moose habitat and to regulate human interactions with moose. The moose benefit from this care and attention, and populations increase. A modern anthropological study of hunting and conservation practices of native people from Labrador showed that they were excellent managers of moose. The elders decided the number of moose to be taken, the kind, and the locality. They limited the kill, and when there were too few moose available, they sent their young people into the cities to work. This is but one example of the wider principle: moose thrive where they are important to people. If

ABOVE: A cow ducks below the water for food, raising its head to masticate.

LEFT: A bull brings aquatic plants to the surface to masticate and swallow. Moose are concentrate feeders with a small rumen and rapid fermentation of food. They also have a huge liver to break down toxic secondary plant compounds. Moose achieve the highest body growth on a diverse, rather than a monotonous diet. The food intake of moose in summer is prodigious, for moose grow and fatten in this short season.

moose have places to live, if there are limits to how many moose may be killed, and if there are ways to enforce those limits, then moose are astonishingly adaptable to modern times.

Moose are completely dependent on the goodwill of humans, and cannot survive where such sympathy is not forthcoming. They cannot survive hungry people, they cannot survive commerce in their dead bodies, they cannot survive domestication, and—above all—they cannot survive apathy. National parks do not protect them, as too many eager visitors generate traffic flows that literally annihilate moose. Cars and moose are not compatible on roads, nor are moose compatible with snowmobiles on narrow trails. Pleasure-seekers in winter disturb weakened moose, which need every ounce of strength to survive. Outside national parks, dams that flood hundreds of miles of river extinguish winter moose habitat. Seismic lines punched through forests bring in more legal and illegal moose hunters. The moose

suffer unless there are people who will speak up for them.

Those who care most passionately about moose are—paradoxically—hunters, in particular people who live in wilderness and rural communities and those who depend on moose for food. In Sweden, no fall menu is without a mouthwatering moose dish. The Swedes fence their highways to reduce moose fatalities and design moose-proof cars. Sweden is less than half as large as the Canadian province of British Columbia, but the annual take of moose in Sweden—upward of 150,000—is twice that of the total moose harvest in North America. That is how much the Swedes cherish their moose. Where many people want moose, and want them badly enough to speak up for them in the political process, moose thrive. The support for moose must come from the population as a whole. In totalitarian regimes, where moose are protected for the pleasure of the elite, they risk being exterminated should

Life eventually ends. The skull of a bull moose in Maine slowly decays, giving off nutrients to surrounding plants and microorganisms.

140

the elite lose power. This is a bitter lesson from over one thousand years of wildlife conservation history.

We are nearing the end of our current interglacial period, and a few cold and warm spells, each lasting a few hundred to a thousand years, are likely to herald in the next continental glaciation. Whatever climatic changes are in store, be they glaciations or global warming, there are more immediate threats to be concerned about. Foremost among these is the rapid growth of the human population, which is expected to peak less than a human lifetime hence. Whatever survives the overcrowding, destruction, and pollution of this time of crisis is likely to be safe. An earth depleted of humans is likely, as is an earth with a badly damaged surface and badly damaged waters and biota. Consequently, we should now be gathering species and ecosystems in a latter-day Noah's Ark, for they will be needed for the great recovery beyond. The better we conserve today, the better the new beginning tomorrow.

These unpleasant thoughts are not for timid souls, but they are necessary. Yet we need not despair. A century ago American wildlife was all but gone. The bleached bones of buffalo were being gathered by the boxcar full to be shipped to eastern kilns. The prairie was empty. Passenger pigeons and Eskimo curlews were on their way to extinction. A few scattered elk survived, but most were protected by the U.S. Army in national parks. Pronghorn, mountain sheep, wood duck, and wild turkeys appeared to be heading the way of the passenger pigeon. Deer were universally depleted. Songbirds were celebrated dishes in expensive restaurants. For those Americans and Canadians who had seen America's glorious wildlife but a few decades earlier, these were times of gloom and anguish; fortunately, they translated their pain into action. Overshadowed by World War I was the birth of North America's continental system of wildlife conservation. It was a system far ahead of its time—and it worked. Wildlife recovered. Species once barely alive flourished. All this on a continent where guns outnumber big game eight to one even today.

The return of North American wildlife from near extinction at the turn of the century is the greatest environmental success story there is. It is also an economic miracle, because publicly owned and managed wildlife has proven itself to be a great creator of wealth and employment. In the United States, expenditures for hunting, fishing, and viewing of wildlife add up to some $60 billion annually, or over $16,500 per square mile ($6,500 per km^2). Just as the publicly funded road system allows the car manufacturers to prosper, so publicly funded wildlife resources benefit private business. In the wildlife sector, about fifty thousand jobs are generated per billion dollars of throughput.

Americans pioneered the creation of national parks and monuments, of federal national forests, and of a wildlife refuge system with over five hundred refuges. Together with Canadians, they pioneered before and during World War I a continental system of wildlife conservation and international wildlife treaties. Leading citizens in both nations worked hard on behalf of wildlife. Their genius was to generate a system of wildlife conservation that was not only endorsed by the blue-collar segment of North American society, but also adopted by it. The public ownership of wildlife is taken very seriously in the United States today, and infractions of wildlife conservation laws are serious offenses.

Science was enshrined as a guide to proper public wildlife management. This was known as the Roosevelt Doctrine. Within a decade, this doctrine led to the creation of a uniquely North American profession, the wildlife biologist. The wildlife we enjoy today has been restored through active, intelligent management. It is not nature's gift. Conservation does work.

We need not despair. We need to be active. History is the best inoculation against bad ideas, but only history squarely faced. Americans three generations ago labored and sacrificed, spurred on by the wish that their children and their children's children might have wildlife to enjoy. Thanks to their generosity and labor, we enjoy wildlife today. Do we dare do less for the future?

Annotated Bibliography

The most comprehensive technical book on moose, *Ecology and Management of the North American Moose*, was compiled and edited by Albert W. Franzmann and Charles C. Schwartz as a Wildlife Management Institute Book published in 1997 by the Smithsonian Institution Press. The book was written by scientists for scientists, but it is rich in detail and data and rewarding for those who can interpret such. It focuses only on moose in North America.

As a bonus, Franzmann and Schwartz's book was illustrated by the late William D. Berry, whose little book *Deneki, An Alaskan Moose* (The Macmillan Company, New York, 1965) is a treasure of superb sketches and keen field observations set outside Mt. McKinley National Park in Alaska. Berry's book is for lay audiences; I cannot praise it highly enough.

An up-to-date synthesis of moose biology is found in chapter nine of *Deer of the World* by Valerius Geist (Stackpole Books, Mechanicsburg, PA, and Airlife Publishing Ltd., Shrewsbury, Great Britain). A fine small book is Douglas B. Houston's *The Shiras Moose in Jackson Hole, Wyoming* (Grand Teton Natural History Association, Technical Bulletin No. 1, 1968). A book still useful is Randolph L. Peterson's *North American Moose* (University of Toronto Press, 1955). Moose biology for laypeople is discussed by Valerius Geist in *Grzimek's Encyclopedia of Mammals*, Vol. 5, pages 229–242 (McGraw Hill, New York, 1990).

Since moose are circumpolar in distribution, there is a considerable amount of literature about moose from German, Scandinavian, and Russian sources. An excellent Russian source, now available in English thanks to the translation by the Translation Publishing Program and editing by Dr. Robert S. Hoffmann of the Smithsonian Institution, is the venerable *Mammals of the Soviet Union*, Vol. 1, by V. G. Heptner, A. A. Nasimovich, and A. G. Bannikov. This excellent book is available from the National Technical Information Service, Springfield, VA 22161, under Technical Translation No. 76-52040. The original Russian version was published in 1961. The edited moose chapter from this book has also been published in German, under the names W. G. Heptner and A. A. Nasimowitsch, as *Der Elch* (Neue Brehm-Bücherei No. 386, A. Ziemsen, Wittenberg-Lutherstadt, 1967).

A more recent source on the Scandinavian moose and its management is *Das Elchwild* by Johnny Rülcker and Finn Stålfelt (P. Parey Verlag, Hamburg, 1986). The Swedish classic on moose is F. Skunke's *Älgen. Studier, jakt och vard* (P. A. Norstedt och Söners förlag, Stockholm, 1949).

An excellent book in German about moose observed year-round in northern Canada is *Goldgelbes Herbstlaub* by Reinhold Eben-Ebenau (P. Parey Verlag, Hamburg, 1953). Eben-Ebenau's passion for moose was matched by keen observations and a sharp, critical mind. Highly recommended! A useful book in German about Alaska moose is *Jagdparadies Alaska* by Ottokar J. Skal (Leopold Stocker Verlag, Graz, Austria, 1982). Another German book by a sharp-witted hunter naturalist, but about Norwegian moose, is *Im Banne des Nordlichts* by Otto Schulz (Verlag J. Neumann-Neudamm, 1931). The history of resurrecting damaged moose populations in East Prussia is recorded by Hans Kramer in *Elchwald* (BLV Verlagsgesellschaft, Munich, 1963). It is an important book that describes how mismanaged moose populations were returned to normalcy.

Recent information on moose is provided by scientific journals such as the *Journal of Wildlife Management*, *Wildlife Monographs*, and *Alces*, and also by periodic international conferences dedicated to moose. The proceedings of one such conference were edited by Dr. Jean Bedard, titled *Alces, Moose Ecology*, and published by *Le Naturalist Canadien* (Vol. 101, Les Presses de L'Université Laval, Quebec, 1974). Another set of proceedings were edited by Görgen Göransson and Sten Lavsund and published in two volumes by *Viltrevy* as supplement No. 1 (1987). It is entitled merely *Proceedings Second International Moose Symposium*; it is available from the *Svenska Jagareforbundet*, Stockholm, Sweden.

Index

About the Author and Photographer

Valerius Geist's career as a zoologist has taken him to many wild places and to meet many of the world's great naturalists. He spent nearly two years in isolation in northern Canada studying mountain sheep and goats, living in a small cabin and not seeing another human being for months on end.

His studies have focused on how animals communicate, the nature of aggression, and status displays, and his mountain sheep work has become well known. His interests extended to the evolution of Ice Age mammals, and later to humans, when he became the first Program Director of Environmental Science in a new Faculty of Environmental Design at the University of Calgary, Alberta, Canada. There he focused on generating environments that maximize human health and developed a biological theory of health. He continued to be interested in wild creatures, but turned from academic to applied science and to wildlife conservation policy.

After twenty-seven years as a professor, Valerius retired to pursue his other interests and to enjoy family life. He and his wife, Renate, have three children and two grandchildren.

Valerius Geist is also the author of *Buffalo Nation: History and Legend of the North American Bison* (published by Voyageur Press), *Mule Deer Country, Elk Country, Wild Sheep Country,* and *Mountain Sheep,* for which he won the 1972 Book of the Year Award from The Wildlife Society. His most recent book, *Deer of the World,* won the prestigious 1999 Literature Prize of the *Conseil International de la Chasse.* He has been a consultant to the National Geographic Society on several books and television specials.

Michael H. Francis is a Montana-based, internationally recognized wildlife photographer whose work has appeared in dozens of books and magazines. His images have appeared in the Voyageur Press books *A Wilderness Called Grand Canyon, Black Bear: Seasons in the Wild, Buffalo Nation, Grizzly Bears, Eagles: Masters of the Sky, Majestic Whitetails, Majestic Elk,* and many others. Moose is the fourth book that Michael H. Francis and Valerius Geist have collaborated on.

Michael H. Francis (Photograph © Bill Silliker, Jr.)